Software
Assistance *for*
Business
Re-
Engineering

Software
Assistance *for*
Business
Re-
Engineering

Edited by

Kathy Spurr
Analysis Design Consultants, UK
Chairman, BCS CASE Specialist Group

Paul Layzell
UMIST, Manchester, UK

Leslie Jennison
TI Information Engineering UK Ltd, UK

Neil Richards
Neil Richards and Company, UK

JOHN WILEY & SONS
Chichester · New York · Brisbane · Toronto · Singapore

Chapter 6 © 1994 Praxis plc
Chapter 8 © 1994 Logica Cambridge Ltd
Chapter 5: copyright in illustrations is owned by EDS Inc., who grant permission
for their publication to John Wiley & Sons Ltd.
Chapter 11, Figure 2: adapted with permission of The Free Press, a division of
Macmillan, Inc. from *Competitive Advantage: Creating and Sustaining Superior
Performance* by Michael E. Porter. Copyright © 1985 by Michael E. Porter

Reprinted July 1994

Other Wiley Editorial Offices

John Wiley & Sons, Inc., 605 Third Avenue,
New York, NY 10158–0012, USA

Jacaranda Wiley Ltd, 33 Park Road, Milton,
Queensland 4064, Australia

John Wiley & Sons (Canada) Ltd, 22 Worcester Road,
Rexdale, Ontario M9W 1L1, Canada

John Wiley & Sons (SEA) Pte Ltd, 37 Jalan Pemimpin #05-04,
Block B, Union Industrial Building, Singapore 2057

British Library Cataloguing in Publication Data

A catalogue record for this book is available from the British Library

ISBN 0 471 94240 5

Typeset in 10/12pt Palatino from author's disks by Text Processing Department,
John Wiley & Sons Ltd, Chichester
Printed and bound in Great Britain by
Biddles Ltd, Guildford and King's Lynn

Contents

Introduction

Being good in business is the most fascinating kind of art.
  Andy Warhol, in *The Observer*, 1 March 1987

WHAT IS BUSINESS RE-ENGINEERING?

Back not so long ago in time, business life proceeded at a slower and simpler pace than it does now. Craftsmen and craftswomen were part of a cottage industry culture which made products to be sold for tokens or traded in exchange for other goods. The driving forces behind any business operation were to survive and to keep the customer happy. Not, as now, to ensure that this year's profit should be bigger than last year's in order to satisfy the demands of the accountant and shareholders. Nor, as in some large, monolithic corporations, to generate just the right amount of paperwork and bureaucracy to keep one's immediate line manager happy. The paying customer used to be at the forefront of the business. If the customer was dissatisfied with the product, then they wouldn't buy it.

Somewhere in the historical development of large corporations, the paying customer seems to have taken on less significance. Businesses have evolved into much larger corporate bodies and have generated their own internal entropy and inefficiencies, often with the result that the goals and purpose of the business have become confused by internal policies and operations. Employees lose sight of essential business goals and their energy is targeted towards competing amongst each other instead of targeting external business opportunities. Internal procedures may have become overburdened by unnecessary paperwork and bureaucracy. This is how a business generates inefficiency. However, the success of a business must be measured in terms of the quality and quantity of the products it sells, rather than how "hard" the employees seem to be working, or how well-documented their internal procedures may be. Purposeful productivity is much more beneficial than purposeless activity or inertia.

Business Re-Engineering (BRE) has become an important discipline which may be applied at several levels within the business. It is necessary to examine the strategic goals of the business, as well as tactical plans and operational implementations. By investigating all these aspects, businesses may be re-engineered to retarget the business itself, to restructure the business or simply to eliminate unnecessary overheads and inefficiencies, with the result that the overall business may be leaner and fitter, enabling those within the business to target their actions more closely towards the paying customer.

Business Re-Engineering encourages us to take another look at the business and to eliminate unnecessary waste in terms of personnel, procedures or resources. It also encourages us to investigate the applicability of new technology (for example groupware, electronic mail) as a mechanism for proactively enhancing and improving the operation of the business.

WHO SHOULD READ THIS BOOK?

This book is of interest to:

- managers and consultants concerned with improving business operations, whether at a strategic, tactical or operational level
- business professionals of any discipline who may wish to apply their experience to business re-engineering
- IT practitioners who need to become effective contributors to business re-engineering projects or implementation
- developers and vendors of tools for business re-engineering, who need to understand the requirements and evolution of this growing market
- lecturers and students in business and computer studies who wish to understand the interplay of business need, techniques and tools in this key field of study.

WHAT DOES THIS BOOK CONTAIN?

This book is based on papers presented at a one day seminar on business re-engineering, held on 29th June 1993 at the National Liberal Club in London. Since the current application of business re-engineering is still very much in its infancy, the seminar was treated as a learning experience for both the presenters and the seminar delegates. The seminar was accompanied by an exhibition of software tools for business re-engineering, details of which appear in this book.

Following the seminar, the presenters were given the opportunity to amend their papers before final publication, based on the discussions which took place. This book contains these amended papers, together with some commentary provided by the editors and summaries of discussions which took place. The seminar ended with a panel session, where the audience was asked to contribute questions and opinions on the subject of business re-engineering. Some of these questions were hard-hitting and indicated a sceptical but optimistic view of the emergent discipline. A report of the panel session is presented.

This book reflects the thoughts and experience of re-engineering practitioners. Some are independent consultants, others represent some of the leading providers of business re-engineering services. They can guide us to some stimulating ideas and research. Though they shared many opinions on the techniques and business environment in which business re-engineering is performed, they were not afraid to be controversial about the use of tools, and the relationship business re-engineering has with information technology.

FORMAT OF THE BOOK

The format of the book broadly reflects that of the seminar, following the themes shown below:

Section 1: How can we re-engineer the business?

Section 2: Does it help to have methods and tools for business re-engineering?

Section 3: How can we make business re-engineering work? (An account of the panel session appears at the end of this section)

Section 4: Some tools for business re-engineering

Commentary has been provided by the editors on each section.

THE BRITISH COMPUTER SOCIETY CASE GROUP

The seminar was organised by the British Computer Society CASE specialist group, formed in 1989, as an independent, non-partisan forum for debate on CASE (Computer Assisted Software Engineering) and related issues. The group felt that it was an appropriate time to hold this seminar, because business re-engineering tools have been emerging which are capable of working with CASE tools, and we wanted to clarify the position of software tools in the business re-engineering cycle.

This is the third set of conference proceedings which have been published on behalf of the BCS CASE specialist group by John Wiley and Sons. The first two volumes, "CASE on Trial" (1990) and "CASE: Current Practice, Future Prospects" (1992), dealt more directly with software engineering. This book continues the theme of software assistance for analytical techniques, but is directed much more towards techniques for analysis of the business rather than the production of a software solution. This theme has cropped up in the previous two volumes, in papers by Fairbairn (CASE on Trial, 1990), and Reynolds and Kalra (CASE: Current Practice, Future Prospects, 1992). For this book, it is not a necessary prerequisite to have read the previous two volumes.

ABOUT THE TITLE OF THIS BOOK

As seminar organisers, one of our crucial decisions related to the title of the seminar and this book of proceedings. This proved not to be trivial. Many terms are currently in use: for example, Business Process Re-Engineering (BPR), Business Engineering (BE), Business Re-Engineering (BRE), Business Process Engineering (BPE). Some contributors to our seminar felt that "business processes" were an important consideration. Others disagreed, preferring to focus less on the business processes and more on strategy, goals and customer value chains. Each of the contributors to this book has used their own terminology, and we have respected their opinions accordingly.

We wondered whether it was better to use a generic term "engineering", rather than "re-engineering", presuming that the former embraced the latter. However, there appeared to be general agreement that "re-engineering" a business was more likely to occur than "engineering" a business from scratch. This is, of course, in contrast to software engineering, which generally applies to the design of a totally new software system.

From our choice, we aimed to achieve a generic title which would encompass the variety of opinions presented in this book, but at the same time convey the very special strengths of this book which touch on software development practices. We hoped to avoid excessive attachment to either "processes", "goals" or "business objects", believing that these and other aspects are all important for business re-engineering, so it would be unfair to mark out any one for special attention. We hope the title we have chosen conveys the content appropriately.

WHAT DOES BUSINESS RE-ENGINEERING MEAN FOR THE SOFTWARE DEVELOPMENT PRACTITIONER?

Since the activities of the BCS CASE group centre mainly around software production, one of the important issues raised by this book must concern the likely impact of business re-engineering on software development, and on participating developers.

Traditionally, systems analysts have had an involvement in the redesign of businesses, as part of the development of a new software system. A key difference now is that perhaps a more systematic approach is being taken to process design and modelling from the management and user perspective, which may force software practitioners to learn new ways of interacting with users. There is also greater pressure to make changes to software production happen more quickly in response to business changes. So software developers also need to learn how to re-engineer their own business practices!

There are many questions to which we do not have all the answers just yet. In particular, it still remains an issue as to where business re-engineering stops, and where software production may begin. In this sense, the overlap between business re-engineering tools and CASE tools is still a little fuzzy (you will notice the variety of opinions presented by the contributors to this book).

Another key question concerns the place of business re-engineering methods and tools within the traditional organisation hierarchy. There appears to be a variety of opinions as to whether business re-engineering should apply to the strategic, tactical or operational levels of the hierarchy. A range of differing opinions are expressed by contributors.

In this book, we don't claim to provide all the answers to these and other questions, but we hope that the book can help you formulate a framework in your own search for answers. Business re-engineering is such a new area that there are still many questions to be raised and answered.

THANK YOU

The editors would like to thank those authors who submitted papers for the seminar. In all cases, the authors had to work to very tight deadlines, in order to meet the publication date. Thanks also to Malcolm Peltu for his critical but valuable comments on this introduction. Finally, thanks to the staff at John Wiley & Sons who were able to re-engineer their publications process in response to the numerous requests we had from seminar delegates for an early publication date following the seminar.

Kathy Spurr
Paul Layzell
Leslie Jennison
Neil Richards
June 1993

Authors' Addresses

EDITORS

Kathy Spurr

Analysis Design Consultants
Lyndhurst Lodge
41 Lyndhurst Road
Chichester
West Sussex
PO19 2LE

Paul Layzell

Department of Computation
UMIST
PO Box 88
Manchester
M60 1QD

Leslie Jennison

Frogmore House
Market Place
Box
Corsham
Wilts SN14 9NZ

Neil Richards

Neil Richards and Company
Hobbits
Danesbury Park Road
Welwyn
Herts
AL6 9SS

AUTHORS

Gary Born

European Business Consulting Group
EDS-Scicon
Pembroke House
Pembroke Broadway
Camberley
Surrey
GU15 3XD

Michael Dale

The Old Windmill
Withybed Lane
Inkberrow
Worcs
WR7 4JL

Faramarz Farhoodi

Logica Cambridge Ltd
Betjemen House
104 Hills Road
Cambridge
CB2 1LQ

Chris Haynes

AT&T ISTEL
PO Box 5
Grosvenor House
Prospect Hill
Redditch
B97 4QD

Linda Hickman

Oracle Corporation UK Ltd
Oracle Park
Bittams Lane
Chertsey
Surrey
KT16 9RG

John Higgins

Nolan and Norton
8 Salisbury Square
London
EC4Y 8BB

Tim Huckvale and
Martyn Ould

Praxis plc
20 Manvers Street
Bath
BA1 1PX
(Praxis is the software engineering
company of Touche Ross Management
Consultants)

Michael Mills and
Clive Mabey

TI Information Engineering UK Ltd
Wellington House
61–73 Staines Road West
Sunbury-on-Thames
TW16 7AH

Chris Moss

Softlab Limited
Axis Centre
3 Burlington Lane
London
W4 2TH

Richard W. Stevenson

COGNITUS Systems Ltd
1 Park View
Harrogate
North Yorkshire
HG1 5LY

Julian Watts

James Martin and Co.
11 Windsor Street
Chertsey
Surrey
KT16 8AY

Trademarks

AIX and RS/6000 are trademarks and DB/2, IBM and OS/2 are registered trademarks of International Business Machines Corporation

Apple is a registered trademark and Macintosh is a trademark of Apple Computer Inc.

Business Design Facility, BDF, Information Engineering Facility, IEF are trademarks and MAXIMIS is a registered trademark of Texas Instruments Inc.

Excel and Windows are trademarks and Microsoft is a registered trademark of Microsoft Corporation

Frame Maker is a trademark of Frame Technology Corporation

HP700 is a trademark of Hewlett-Packard Company

Interleaf is a trademark of Interleaf Inc.

ithink is a trademark of High Performance Systems Inc.

Object Management Workbench and Kappa are trademarks of Intellicorp Inc.

ProcessWise is a registered trademark of International Computers Limited

SPARC is a trademark of SPARC International Inc.

StP and Software thru Pictures are tradmarks of IDE

Sun is a trademark of Sun Microsystems Inc.

STRIM is a registered trademark of Praxis Systems plc

Teamwork is a trademark of CADRE Technologies, Inc.

TOPFLOW, TOPGEN, TOP-IX, TOPMAN, and TOPLAN are trademarks of TOP-IX Limited

ULTRIX and VMS are trademarks of Digital Equipment Corporation

UNIX is a trademark of UNIX System Laboratories Inc.

X/Open is a trademark of X/Open Company Limited

X Vision is a trademark of Visionware Limited

Section 1

How Can We Re-engineer the Business?

Neil Richards

What is Business Re-Engineering (BRE)? The three authors in this section describe it as a process by which companies can ascertain the value and effectiveness of their current business processes against their customers' assessment. It covers what the organisation does and how it does it. BRE is generally accompanied by a major cultural change to the organisation. A BRE project can range from simplifying certain activities, through re-engineering certain processes, to re-engineering the entire business.

What are business processes? Business processes are sets of logically related tasks or activities, linked together by flows of information or materials, by which an organisation achieves its business results. They exist throughout the life of the product or service, from creation, through production, to order delivery and after-service.

How should the change to the organisation be managed? BRE, as has been stated earlier, is concerned with substantial change to an organisation. Such change creates conflict. Conflict can be positive (if it builds a better result than would have been the case had the conflict not been present) or negative (if it tends to destroy what has been done). Consequently, change management is of major importance. Mike Dale states that the

Software Assistance for Business Re-engineering. Edited by Kathy Spurr, Paul Layzell, Leslie Jennison and Neil Richards
© 1993 John Wiley & Sons Ltd

re-engineering process will create "issues" which will need to be resolved. Indeed, he believes that resolution workshops need to be held for the benefit of the workforce to explain why the issues were solved in the way they were. According to John Higgins, this is an essential part of his "Rollout" phase.

When and how should Business Re-Engineering be used? Companies should only choose to use a Business Re-Engineering approach when they wish to be innovative. BRE is not necessarily based on any "existing system". Indeed Dale questions whether there is any need to analyse the current system at all before suggesting a new design. Both he and Higgins recommend the use of prototyping tools to gain the creativity necessary for this innovation. Chris Haynes also suggests that synthesis and intuition are as important as the traditional system development activities of analysis and rule-making.

How should the objectives of a BRE project be derived? It is generally agreed by the three authors that, because a BRE project seeks to improve the service to the eventual customer, it should not be seen as an object in its own right but rather as a part of the company's search for quality improvement. They all believe that a BRE project should not, indeed cannot, be performed as just another type of Information Systems project. It has be a high profile, company-wide activity. Therefore it needs inputs from different schools of thought. Haynes states that these inputs should come from four sources: the graduates of business schools, the analysts and designers from the Information Systems department, the technocrats who know the state-of-the-art of Information Technology (IT), and the company's line management. Dale generally agrees with these input sources but adds another, that of the Human Resources development function.

How should the BRE team be structured and what implications are there on the Information Systems department? The structure of the BRE team is discussed by all three authors. Higgins states that the BRE project should have an executive business champion to ease any organisational politics. Dale also sees it being run as a "business" project with a top management sponsor, a core team and co-opted specialists. These specialists would be assigned from such functions as Information Systems, Training, etc. Haynes believes that line management plays an essential role in the composition of any BRE team. His point is that, because the whole objective of BRE is to help line management improve their operation, they must be fully involved in the team. The competence of the Information Systems Department (ISD) to support the technological and systems infrastructure necessary to underpin a BRE exercise is discussed by both Higgins and Haynes. Higgins argues that the success rate for the ISD implementing systems needs to be reviewed before a company embarks on a BRE project.

Too many well-designed systems are failing to be implemented. This is because the "people issues" in information systems are mostly ignored, according to the results of a study he quotes. He also argues that, if the ISD is wrongly structured, it can negate the benefits that ought to be realised from BRE. It is essential for it to appreciate the business priorities of the various candidate projects it has to select from, and choose the correct ones. Haynes also cites the "applications backlog" which adds massively to the delays and risks in selecting the right projects to initiate.

How can the success of a BRE project be measured? BRE should create realisable benefits. Dale sees the project linked in some way to the strategic planning of the company. Higgins sees it as part of the company's operational plan. Both agree that the benefits should be identifiable and measurable, and their attainment capable of being scheduled in a plan.

What methodologies and tools should be used with BRE? Higgins believes that the use of current methodologies in the area of innovative systems could become a straight-jacket. Haynes draws attention to the fact that three sets of people currently work with business processes, each with different aims. As well as BRE practitioners there are line managers, who need tools to describe the business processes in their quality-related process management, and IS personnel who use methods/tools when analysing and designing the information systems components of business processes. He argues that it would be dangerous for BRE practitioners to use these existing tools and methodologies as BRE work is fundamentally different from the design work carried out for information- or quality-related systems, which are relatively static. BRE, he argues, is not concerned with functional organisation design, as used by the other disciplines, but with the value perceived by the customer. For this reason it is necessary that new supporting methodologies and tools be made available for the BRE practitioner.

1

Business Re-Engineering: The Business Realities

Michael W Dale

ABSTRACT

This paper discusses some of the strategic and organisational aspects of business process re-engineering. Terms are defined to distinguish between process simplification and process re-engineering. Two schools of process re-engineering are identified, namely the Quality School and the Information School. The nature and implications of radical change are described including difficulties peculiar to process re-engineering. Requirements for successfully organising design work are set out including the skill specification of an important role, namely that of the Systems Engineer. Some approaches for handling change are described, including both encouraging and managing the positive tensions that arise during the change. A distinction is drawn between the meeting of specifications and satisfying the expectations of managers and users. Challenges and recommendations are posed to the Information Systems function in businesses. Conclusions are drawn about the factors which make up a successful re-engineering change programme.

Software Assistance for Business Re-engineering. Edited by Kathy Spurr, Paul Layzell, Leslie Jennison and Neil Richards
© 1993 John Wiley & Sons Ltd

INTRODUCTION

This paper takes a broad business view of business re-engineering. Its purpose is to enable those who work on the technologies that help re-engineering work and on the information systems which embody business processes to relate their work to the wider picture.

WHAT IS RE-ENGINEERING?

Business process re-engineering means many things to many people. It ranges in scope from process simplification, in which the task is essentially to improve significantly what already exists, to process re-engineering which reconceptualises how "door to door" business processes work, i.e. processes which traverse the organisation from one external boundary to another. Beyond even that is business re-engineering, whereby the business itself is reconceptualised including its relationship with its customers or suppliers. Probably the best known example of this is First Direct, where not only have the internal workings of the business been engineered from zero base but also the route to market and the way of working with the customer, by telephone, is different as well. We do not need to examine the relatively few examples of business re-engineering, however, to gain insight into what the subject is about and how to make it successful. Figure 1 illustrates schematically a flow chart which was drawn of the process for turning enquiries into quotations for a medium sized business which designs and makes electronic sub-assemblies. The business is in batch manufacture serving several market sectors. There is a significant volume of traffic flowing down the process and the business was suffering from slow and unreliable turn-round times on quotations. The field salesmen were turning up the opportunities but some were being lost due to quotation turn-round times that were unpredictable and longer than the industry norm.

As indicated in the figure, the team which worked on this project considered that there were only 6 useful operations carried out in this process in the sense that they directly contributed to the task of preparing the quotation for the customer. There were 14 transfers between departments, the points where errors and delays are most likely to occur. This goes some way to explaining the astonishing amount of checking which took place, much of it checking internal administration tasks. This project was done some time ago and the flow charting technique used was very simple; that is not a pejorative statement because it enabled the business to address and solve its business problem.

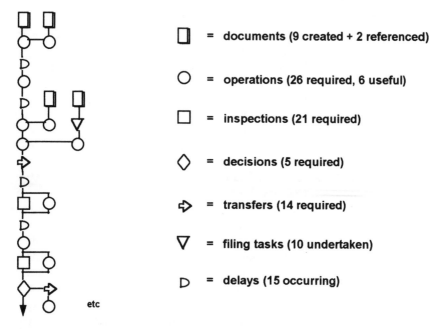

Figure 1   Flow chart for preparing quotations

The solution chosen was a process simplification one. The process was cleaned up and streamlined by cutting out some of the no-value-added tasks. Clearer distinctions were made between the processes for different types of quotations, for example repeat enquiries, new variations of standard products and new custom designed products which needed a full engineering proposal. Some people who used to work in different departments were moved into an open plan office working for one manager. The number of managers was reduced. This team then had control of 85% of the process. The changes were made within weeks and the turn-round time on quotations rapidly fell to a reliable and acceptable level.

This is an easy to explain and classic example of process simplification. It has the hallmark of good work in this field by having at its root a few simple ideas which are easy to understand. It contains three very common general concepts of process redesign, viz.:

- Waste elimination;
- Workflow classification;
- Clustering into Natural Groups.

The simplification solution chosen cost little more than the time of the people involved, a few man weeks of consultancy time and an office reorganisation. The payback was within a few months.

The business might have chosen a re-engineering solution where the field salesmen were equipped with portable computers which contain the systems and data that enable them to deal with all but those quotations requiring a full engineering proposal. This would not have been straightforward, however, as it is not only specifications, prices and commercial terms which have to be offered but also delivery dates which depend on load, capacity and schedule in a high variety make-to-order factory. It would also have taken a lot longer and required a much bigger investment and contained greater risks.

There is another difference between the simplification solution chosen and the re-engineering one which other businesses in a comparable position have implemented. The simplification solution comes from what can be called the Quality School of process re-engineering; this tends to concentrate on workflows, quality, value added and people. It should not be confused with the installation of an ISO 9000 quality system which cements quality procedures into the business. The potential high technology solution comes from what we can call the Information School of process re-engineering; this tends to concentrate more on information flows, data, systems and technology. The best re-engineering work contains elements of both. So to gain the benefits of the more expensive re-engineering solution in this example would have required a similar activity to reconceptualise the process, remove waste and change the organisation as well as the investment in information technology.

So what is required is a well rounded approach, in fact a holistic approach, not just in the thinking and planning but also in the implementation. So business process re-engineering must address:

- The reconceptualisation of the process;

- The embodiment of the new process in policies, systems, etc.;

- The management of all the project tasks;

- The management of the organisational and personal change.

In addition, re-engineering sometimes also involves changes to the offerings made to the market and their positioning.

RADICAL CHANGE

Even with process simplification and certainly with re-engineering, the changes made to a business are radical. The ideas may be simple with the benefit of hindsight but for the people in the business it can be a dramatic change which affects them personally. Reporting relationships change. Job roles and skill requirements differ. The changes are in fact outside the current rules of the game, many people actively disagreeing with them. The disagreement may be because they feel personally threatened or because they believe passionately that incorrect decisions have been made. Either way, many will be taken outside their own personal comfort zones which causes disfunctional feelings and behaviours. So re-engineering processes mean we are dealing with:

• Personal interests;
• Values and beliefs held within the business;
• Power structures;
• Bureaucratic inertia.

All this adds up to mean that the change is transformational. Whether or not the business performance or the nature of the business ends up being transformed, for the people affected it is a transformational change. Transformational change is complex and difficult to manage.

Good practice in change management tells us to involve from the start those who will be affected by the changes in order to get their ownership and commitment; so we should get those who will be working the process to be involved in the design and implementation planning. In the case of re-engineering changes this may not be straightforward because the process changes will cause changes to roles, jobs and skills. Good practice in organisation design therefore says we should select people for the new roles and jobs to ensure a match between people and job requirements. This means that it may not be clear who will be in the jobs until implementation is in progress.

From these illustrations it should be clear that business process re-engineering inevitably involves a complex change management programme, both organisational change and personal change. Many would say that this is half of the project, sometimes more. What must also be realised is that personal and organisational change is not just a matter for people at the "doing" end of the organisation but also for those in the higher echelons too. However, in the upper parts of the organisation, the stakes are higher, the power plays more significant, and the beliefs and behaviours more ingrained. After all, what made these people succeed in progressing up the organisation in the past was that they excelled at the old rules of the game.

In more than one business, members of the top management team have been asked to leave at a point in the re-engineering when it was not only apparent that did they not support the new ways of working but that they could not be persuaded. Sometimes this is because they are locked into mental models and behaviour habits; and in one business, the senior team undertook a programme of team development work to help with the behaviours but still had difficulties because their mental models and goals were not genuinely shared.

ORGANISING FOR DESIGN

Some things are clear about how to organise business process re-engineering projects. They must be run as a business project, not an information systems project. There must be a very senior sponsor whose role has been legitimised by all the other senior stakeholders in whose turf the project will operate. A core team is required during the early stages to do analysis work and to design the proposed new process. This is not an information systems team but a multi-disciplinary team whose real leader (not just a figurehead) is a business manager involved with the current process and who has the essential street credibility. It is likely that team members will be those whom it is difficult to release because of their skills or their standing. The core team should contain within its membership:

- All the business disciplines which are relevant to the business process;
- Owners of the relevant business activities;
- Creativity, insight and intuition;
- Experience and innocence;
- Analytical, project management and teamwork skills;
- A balance of teamworking skills.

The last point about teamworking can easily be dealt with by use of Belbin's work on team roles. The core team is invariably supplemented by a wider team of people who manage parts of the current process, who are "do-ers" on the process or who have scarce specialist expertise.

Although analysis is required both to establish what exists and to test hypotheses, the essence of the core task is design. Design is not the same as

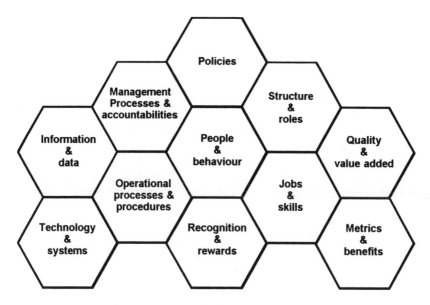

Figure 2   The elements of process design

analysis. It is creative and intuitive. It involves the synthesis of concepts, something that is hardly taught or developed, even in engineering degree courses. Designing business processes needs to integrate all the aspects illustrated in figure 2 including not just the separate elements but also the interactions between the elements. This cannot be done in the deterministic sense that a gearbox or data processing software is designed but nevertheless there is a skilful design job to do.

For this reason, such teams work well if they have a Systems Engineer in their make-up. In this context the ideal Systems Engineer has the following technical/professional skills:

- Systems analysis;
- System dynamics;
- Quality management;
- Organisation and methods;
- Work design;
- Costing;
- Project management;

- Data management;
- Fluent personal computer user to handle analysis and presentation work.

In addition the systems engineer should have process consulting skills as well as being a good challenger, communicator and teamworker. Arguably, a good understanding of strategic management concepts should be added to the list.

It may seem a daunting list but this is the full armoury that is needed to be a really effective process designer and change agent. Others continue to provide specialist expertise of the various sorts whether they be, for example, business, information technology, or human resource development specialisms. Clearly the average member of an Information Systems function does not immediately fit the Systems Engineer profile outlined above and many would not have the personal attributes to do so even with training and development. If Information Systems functions are to play their full part in process re-engineering they need to consider how to fulfil this role and how to acquire and deploy the skills.

The choice of techniques and tools also influences design. For example, using hierarchical decomposition techniques to produce a model of what exists has its dangers. The benefit is to create a comprehensive picture but the risk is to cement mental models of how the processes work now. In inexperienced hands such analysis does not expose the drivers of process performance (lead time, quality, service, cost) and may even obscure business issues. One large manufacturing business based on two sites successfully used hierarchical activity analysis on one site to provide the foundation for plugging gaps in the quality procedures but resisted the temptation on another site of doing a full analysis in the early stages of a business redesign. Instead the big role, relationship, accountability and process issues were resolved first using very basic techniques. Detailed analysis then followed to precede the detailed design.

On the other hand, if radically different systems applications and working practices are envisaged it is extremely helpful to have tools which allow system prototypes to be produced rapidly so that the whole process including systems and jobs can be trialled. It simply isn't feasible to foresee all the requirements; it is asking the impossible for system users to know all that they want before they have experienced what can be done. The implication of this for the Information Systems function is profound. It is not appropriate to have a contractual relationship with other people in the business whereby a complex and detailed specification is presented to the "customer" for him to sign so that the "supplier" can proceed through to implementation in the comfort of knowing that changes have to be negotiated and are the opportunity to change the contract. A flexible and collaborative partnership is needed with a sense of shared destiny.

To help achieve this kind of relationship it is worth recognising that the advances in software development methodologies and CASE tools of recent years have had big benefits in higher productivity, shorter lead time and better conformance to requirements. However, there is more to do; it is also necessary to satisfy expectations. Managers' and users' expectations exist for all sorts of reasons, some easy to understand, others completely obscure. Satisfying expectations, and sometimes managing expectations, is a higher level and more difficult task than meeting specifications. It behoves the Information Systems profession to learn ways to improve further in this area.

ORGANISING FOR CHANGE

The starting point for change is to get people to want to change. Except in a totalitarian environment the notion of changing someone else simply isn't valid; what can be done is to change one's own behaviour in a way which makes the other person interested in learning and wanting to change. In an organisational context, we have the additional levers to pull such as the policies which guide what is done and the financial and other resources that are allocated by choice to different activities.

In the context of business process re-engineering, much needs to be done to create a felt-need for change. Very often this is associated with external threats, such as loss of competitiveness or the reality of moving from public to private sector. Sometimes it stems from the vision of an opportunity. There are obvious things to do like communication and benchmarking, but having the information is not of itself sufficient to cause people to want to change nor organisations to have the capacity for change. The world is replete with corporations which knew about their problems but which were not able to make a fundamental change until the problems called for urgent and drastic action. Additional activities are required to change the way people think and to help them get over the constraint of not knowing what they don't know; so educational and development activities should be used to:

• Give good understanding of the problem;
• Offer new mental models for people to use;
• Expose the opportunities;

- Convince people that there are other ways which work;
- and INVOLVE THEM IN THE PROCESS OF CHANGE.

Even before a re-engineering project gets under way when senior managers are choosing which process to work on and whether to simplify or re-engineer, tensions may emerge. Once into the project others always arise. Some of these tensions are very constructive and should be encouraged both to help the felt-need for change and to help generate a significant improvement in performance. There are tensions between innovation and risk, between core team effectiveness and ownership by those who work in the process, between function and process views of the business. By the choice of the people in the core team and of those in the wider project team who are involved across the business, as well as the way in which the project is led, these tensions can be both encouraged and managed.

Other tensions have their roots in personal or function fears and interests. These and other barriers such as current policies and behavioural habits will cause blockages to thinking and progress. Issues arise for which there is no clear answer but which must be resolved. Contradictions or overlap may appear between the business process re-engineering project and other initiatives.

The core team can handle some of these issues and it is always useful to keep an inventory of outstanding issues, rate them for their significance, action people to pursue their resolution and circulate decisions when they are resolved. Whilst traditional approaches to project management tend to concentrate on the tasks it is at least as important in transformational change to track and manage the issues which are in effect the spaces between the tasks. It is also essential to recognise that there is a much wider and more diffuse project to manage, beyond designing the process and developing systems. Some of this wider project cannot be managed by the core team but rests on the shoulders of the sponsor. The team leader can orchestrate but it may be the sponsor who has the position to get some of the more difficult issues resolved.

As the project progresses through the conceptual work into the implementation phases continual attention is needed to change management. The project team should devote a high proportion of its time to involving the wider business population through communications and issue resolution workshops. Later this should be followed through with roll-out programmes to draw all the process "do-ers" into the activity. They need to feel involved; so this argues for leaving some of the detail to be decided by them. They need the skills; so suitable training activities are required to give competence in the new tasks and in the new behaviours.

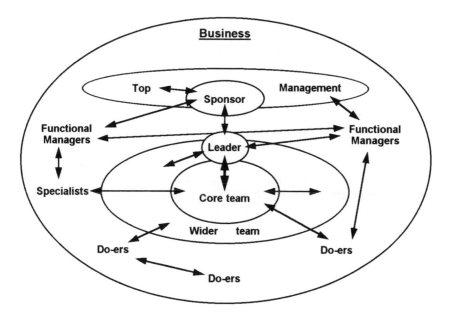

Figure 3 Project interactions

They need to build the confidence to work in the new ways; so support and development activities must also be in place. Figure 3 attempts to represent schematically some of the dynamics and interactions which go on. The intention is to convey an impression of highly interactive working with the team leader at the hub.

Another potential difficulty is when the project goes through any kind of discontinuity. For example, when a process has been selected and a team is to be formed to do the conceptual work; when the work moves from conceptual to detailed work on information systems; when the project moves into physical implementation. At each point like this, new people become involved who may not have been through all the formative steps and who may not have the same commitment. At these points the risks of delay, regression and dilution of intentions are particularly high; so extra attention and reinforcement pays dividends. Smooth transitions across the discontinuities are also helped by ensuring that a minority of the people who have been at the centre of the preceding phase continue to be involved for some time into the following phase. Their continuation may not at first appear justified and adds to the pain of dedicating good people to the re-engineering project but it pays off by preventing loss of momentum or degradation of the vision.

CONCLUSIONS

There are many methodologies, techniques and tools which can be used for re-engineering work. Some are more powerful and useful than others; some can be positively unhelpful if used inappropriately. However, it isn't possible to prescribe a precise method for managing this type of change; indeed the choice of techniques and tools is arguably a second order decision. This is not in any way an argument against the use of software engineering methodologies and CASE tools for embodying the process in new systems applications.

Each circumstance is unique, depending on the business, its history and its culture. It is only possible to identify potential pitfalls and set out principles which will encourage success. It is clear, however, that business process re-engineering projects must be managed as an integrated change programme with:

- Very high level sponsorship;
- Involvement of all affected functions;
- A close alliance between the Information Systems and Human Resource functions;
- Deployment of high calibre resource during both design and implementation;
- People-centred implementation.

Recognising the demands which such a programme has on the business indicates that there is a limit to the number which can be tackled at any one time. This also suggests that it can only really be justified if there is a clear linkage between the programme and the strategic intent with clear criteria for success. For example it would be unfortunate to focus exclusively on cost reduction when the key strategic need was for improvements in service. Expending the amount of energy associated with a true re-engineering project demands repayment by a result which gives measurable leverage on the business strategy. So two other criteria for success are:

- Tight linkage to a clear strategic intent;
- A specific plan for delivery of the identified benefits.

IMPLICATIONS FOR THE INFORMATION SYSTEMS FUNCTION

These conclusions and the supporting arguments set out earlier imply that, in the context of business re-engineering, the Information Systems function should:

- Not regard re-engineering as an IS crusade;
- but ensure that they are included in re-engineering activities;
- Ask difficult questions if the link to strategy is not clear and explicit;
- Review and if necessary adapt their skills base to match the requirements of re-engineering;
- Recognise the existence of the Quality School of re-engineering;
- Recognise that techniques and tools have limitations for *design* of the *process*;
- Establish ways to improve their ability to satisfy expectations.

BIBLIOGRAPHY

Reports:

"Business Re-engineering", by Peter Bartram, published by Business Intelligence.

Books:

"Re-engineering the Corporation", by Michael Hammer and James Champy, published by Brealey;
"Process Innovation", by Thomas Davenport, published by Harvard Business Press.

Papers:

R G Ligus, "Methods to Help Re-engineer Your Company for Improved Agility", Industrial Engineering, January 1993;
J W Verity & G McWilliams, "Is it Time to Junk the Way You Use Computers", Business Week, July 22 1991;
P F Drucker, "The Coming of the New Organisation", Harvard Business Review, Jan/Feb 1988.

2

Information Technology and Business Process Redesign: IT—Enabler or Disabler of BPR

John Higgins

ABSTRACT

Business Process Redesign as a concept is contained within the overall domain of innovation. It focuses on examining how corporate space and time can be redeployed for the benefit of the customer, outside of the traditional, functional paradigm of corporate organisation.

IT is at the heart of the new potential for reorganising how companies work. Too often, however, IT is thought about purely from the perspective of a single function, the technology itself, and with the single goal of automation. As a consequence a deadly embrace has evolved, with IT organisations now geared to fulfilling these limited, uninnovative, business expectations.

The sobering conclusion is that IT cannot be effectively deployed to redesign and re-engineer business processes, until the fundamental

---

Software Assistance for Business Re-engineering. Edited by Kathy Spurr, Paul Layzell, Leslie Jennison and Neil Richards
© 1993 John Wiley & Sons Ltd

relationship between IT and the business community has itself been redefined and re-engineered.

INTRODUCTION

This paper investigates the role that information technology has in helping or hindering organisations which are carrying out "business process redesign".

It is structured so as to:

- Put BPR in context—drawing out what is at its heart, which is a particularly focused form of innovation.
- Provide an overview of innovation and its lifecycle.
- Identify the specific phases of the innovation lifecycle—and their unique characteristics.
- Identify the major roles that IT has in innovation.
- Review the major drivers behind the effective (and ineffective) use of IT in innovation.
- Look at what leads to successful innovation involving IT.

The term BPR is used to cover the full life of process redesign, from original conception through to the new design becoming accepted as business-as-usual. It should therefore, for the sake of this paper and to avoid the semantic disputations which are helping to discredit this field of analysis, be read as synonymous with Business Re-engineering.

PUTTING BPR IN CONTEXT

In many companies Business Process Redesign has been treated as a topic in its own right and touted as the final solution to all business performance problems. Lead times too long? Don't worry, redesign the problem away. Costs too high? Don't forget to redesign. Customer service. . . . The list is as long as the number of issues on the executive agenda.

Misapplied, BPR can become decoupled from the wider business context and the political and cultural realities of an organisation. In particular, as is the focus of this paper, it can become decoupled from an organisation's ability to both demand and supply IT. At its worst, BPR turns into a project in its own right, driven by some management cadre who have a belief in the perfectability of business operations—if only it was possible to remove people from their operations completely. This belief in the perfectability of the world, without people, is also a state of mind not uncommon in the IT community.

The problem with this decoupled BPR is that it runs completely counter to the work done by Deming, Zuboff and others, who emphasise both the importance of institutionalising process improvement by giving staff the power to improve themselves, as well as the need to enrich the work experience so that people stay engaged with their work and the value it creates. Deming is, of course, extremely damning about any abrogation of control to management, as he sees management as the cause of organisational and performance problems in 85% of cases.

Stripping away the hype and the bad practice of treating BPR as an object in its own right, there are a number of significant insights that BPR does provide which are of importance when it comes to thinking about how and where to deploy IT investment.

At its heart, BPR is concerned with focusing on the "customer" (the ultimate end-user) and looking at how an organisation works to meet the needs of its customers. As a consequence of this focus, functional boundaries become subsumed and cross-functional contradictions, inconsistencies and co-ordination issues are highlighted—an important consideration when you bear in mind that Xerox found that over 80% of their operational errors occurred at functional interfaces. The good BPR study will then begin to identify how the company needs to change, to innovate, so as to overcome these functionally induced problems and better service the customer.

In essence BPR is a particular form of innovation, given that innovation is the process of thinking about and identifying how things can be done differently. The twist that BPR adds is the focus it puts on innovation, i.e. a focus on customers and cross-functional issues and the role that IT has in addressing (or underpinning) these issues.

THE INNOVATION LIFECYCLE—OVERVIEW

Since BPR can be seen as a particularly focused form of innovation, this allows us to apply many of the lessons that organisations have already learnt about using IT to do business differently.

An important point to understand about innovation and IT is that the role of IT varies with the innovation lifecycle. This concept of the innovation lifecycle is drawn from work done by my colleague Dr Martin Lockett into "What Makes IT Work?" (published in "Information

Management: The Organisational Dimension", OUP, 1992). He identifies that during the process of innovation, five distinct phases can be identified, as innovation moves from an *identification of need* through *experimentation* to *refocusing* in the light of experience to the *rolling out* and institutionalising of the innovation on a wider basis, before finally getting some real business value from the exercise by actively managing to *get the benefits* that you actually wanted in the first place.

He identifies that as the stage of innovation changes, so must the management approach and analytical techniques that are appropriate. At the start of an innovative project, the need is to be flexible in approach and be content with using the 80:20 rule to focus efforts and attention on those areas of the business that really do have a significant impact on cost, quality and service—thus avoiding the momentum destroying act of mindless comprehensiveness that many "Architectural" methodologies require. As innovation progresses and the objectives become clearer, so there is a need to shift to tighter management approaches and the use of more rigorous and comprehensive analytical techniques, capable of delivering working, practical solutions.

THE FIVE PHASES OF INNOVATION

The diagram below summarises the five phases of innovation.

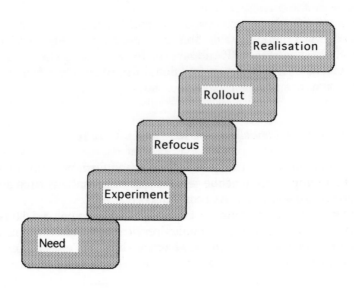

Phase 1—Need. Within the organisation, there must be either a belief in the need for continuous innovation or else a specific issue or pressure that has got change onto the executive agenda. For cross-functional, customer focused innovation, it is almost inevitable that "need" will have to be defined or raised at the board level, so that the review of the problem or opportunity can be legitimised—given that it will inevitably be cutting across functions and baronial empires.

Phase 2—Experiment. This phase is often a perfect example of the dog that didn't bark, in other words noticeable more for its absence than its presence. Many organisations try and leap directly from need identification to definitive solution. This reflects the problems that managers have in any creative work, namely how do you legislate for (and control) what is going on in a person's head? How do you monitor creativity? Given that this phase cannot be managed purely on the basis of input, it is tempting to avoid facing up to the management challenges it presents. It is, however, a vital phase, for it allows mistakes to be made in a controlled environment, whilst at the same time serving as a magnet for attracting ideas and opinions from the organisation as a whole.

Phase 3—Refocus. Experimentation should produce some surprising results. Organisations are organic, not mechanical, therefore new and unexpected non-systemic results are bound to occur when you introduce change. Learning from experimentation, and refocusing priorities in the light of a better understanding of what the organisation can actually achieve, should result in a better understanding of the best way to move forward. In an over-structured approach, organisations cannot learn because boundaries are set too soon and a project takes on a life of its own, divorced from the wider universe of the world at large.

Personal experience in this area also highlights another problem, to do with the hijacking of customer service benefit opportunities by the more bottom line orientated business functions. The US operations of a UK Finance House identified a huge potential improvement in customer service in terms of the time taken to make corporate lending decisions (the scale of improvement was by a factor of 14). An experiment proved the concept, but also identified some very immediate staff cutting opportunities. Given the culture and IT literacy of the management team, they felt much more comfortable making the internal cost cutting move rather than going for the revenue generating "uncertainty" of dramatically improved customer service. As a consequence, the redesign was corrupted into an old fashioned automate to cut headcount, based on the outmoded principle that low cost and high quality service are mutually exclusive.

Phase 4—Rollout. Given the refined objectives and implementation issues that the experimentation phase will have identified, the rollout is the formal implementation and institutionalisation of the innovation within the organisational mainstream. The key factor to bear in mind here is the vital importance of maintaining balance. From the perspective of IT, all too often rollout is seen simply in IT system implementation terms and all the other enabling organisational changes are put on the back burner. This often reflects two factors: firstly IT professionals are good at project management and so produce better plans than their business colleagues—and since they produce the manageable agenda they get all the management attention; secondly the IT system project is the most measurable and most tangible aspect of the change, so it is the easiest for management to keep an eye on.

Phase 5—Realisation. Benefits do not happen by accident. They have to be created and then actively managed, preferably by incorporating them into the existing operational plans that the organisation has in place. In addition to this aggressive harvesting, organisations must remain alert to new and unexpected benefits that the change makes possible. The organisation must also remain alert to the need to reprioritise the benefits given the state of the world as it is, rather than as it was when the change was first mooted.

INNOVATION AND INFORMATION TECHNOLOGY

IT has three major roles in innovation. Firstly it opens up new business opportunities, secondly it provides a platform of systems and capabilities that new working practices can be based on, and thirdly it allows new systems to be put in place.

Role 1—New Business Opportunities. For IT to be of value there must be a business community understanding of what is possible with computer based technologies, or at least a vehicle for effectively educating people in what IT makes possible. Following the Deming philosophy that if you want to know how to improve a job, ask the person who does it at the moment, it is important that this knowledge of the business potential of IT capabilities is not limited to some cadre of experts—especially not IT experts. Broadly IT opportunities can be seen as falling into three areas:

- IT has an industry restructuring potential—as in the example of 7-Eleven Japan, which became a retailer without shops and took over the high ground of retailing, namely the distribution network and the stocking information.

- IT's ability to improve a company's position within an industry—as with Otisline and their ability to manage actively their lift service reliability, to such an extent that they were able to regain market share.

- IT's ability to create new business opportunities—as with Reuters becoming the *de facto* market for certain aspects of financial and equity trading, or even the Japanese creating intelligent washing machines.

Role 2—A Platform of Systems and Capabilities. Many companies do not use their existing systems to anything like their full potential—reflecting a reasonably typical scenario of an IT supply capability exceeding the ability of the user community to use what is available. If an organisation innovates without a clear understanding of what its current IT platform is like, it can miss opportunities it didn't know it had or it can try and run before it can walk—by attempting the innovative use of complex technology when its business and IT management teams are simply not up to the task.

Role 3—Delivering New Systems. Innovation is only of value when something different is done at the end of it. This will frequently require new systems to be in place and the track record of firms' abilities to deliver systems cost-effectively is often poor. Organisations must therefore ensure that they have the skills and management to deliver systems to time, budget and specification—a state of affairs that is markedly easier to talk and write about, than actually achieve.

To successfully integrate IT into cross-functional, customer focused innovation, organisations must actively manage all these three roles of IT.

DRIVERS BEHIND THE (IN)EFFECTIVE USE OF IT IN INNOVATIVE PROJECTS

The effectiveness, or more commonly ineffectiveness, with which IT is used during a redesign programme is driven by four factors:

— the potential of the technology itself,

— the organisational structure and position of the IT department,

— the people, skills and procedures that are in place to deliver IT,

— the existing corporate investment in applications and computer systems.

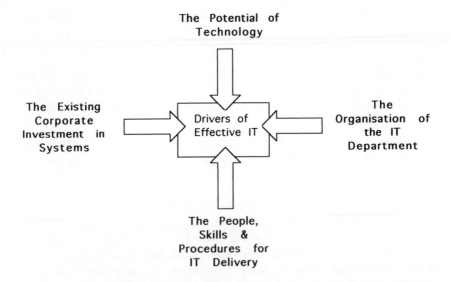

Driver 1—The Potential of Technology Itself. Given the seemingly limitless potential of technology, it is tempting for businessmen to be seduced by the idea that an electronic black box will solve all their problems. In effect there has often been a conspiracy between businessmen and technologists, with businessmen wanting easy answers and technologists willing to peddle them—and even when this isn't the case, business management can sometimes become bewitched by all the gizmos and gee-whizzery and forget to look at the business realities that should be the focus of their attention.

Focus of attention is also at the heart of the second point about the potential of technology. Nolan, Norton & Co. recently carried out interviews with 50 senior IT directors to see what caused them problems in their IT investments—and where the focus of their organisations' planning effort went. 78% of their difficulties came from getting people to use and exploit new systems—only 9% of their problems came from technical problems. Yet 54% of their planning focused purely on technical issues, whilst the people issues received no dedicated planning time at all—and yet it's the people using the technology who actually deliver the business benefit. Managers, no doubt, feel more comfortable with machines, rather than the illogical, emotional human beings who keep failing to behave as they should. The key lessons about effectively harnessing the potential of technology are therefore:

• Don't be seduced by technology.

- Don't put too much effort into managing the purely technological aspects of innovation to the detriment of the people side.

Driver 2—The Organisation of the IT Department. Put bluntly, many IT organisations are still based on a Soviet style command economy. This manifests itself, firstly, in over-centralisation and excessive planning, predicated on a belief that given enough time the world is a totally manageable and modellable entity—a state of mind with which Taylor and the school of scientific management, with its focus on operational decomposition and simplication, would probably agree. Secondly, IT departments still have a tendency to behave as monopoly suppliers, justifying their control of corporate IT resources on the grounds of technical expertise and the need to hoard "scarce" technical skills. To institutionalise this approach, firms still use performance measures that over-focus on technical excellence and bureaucratic hierachies.

In defence of IT departments, this organisational tendency can be seen throughout all departments within many organisations, where the principles of scientific management have been used to justify an organisational structure which has more in common with the communism of Marx and Lenin than the free market principles of Adam Smith. So the IT department is just adapting itself to the prevailing business culture rather than behaving in a uniquely unwieldly way. Despite this caveat, however, many IT departments do seem to behave as if the rules of business don't apply to them and easily forget that technology is not an end in itself. The evidence for this is in the number of projects involving IT which have only a tenuous business rationale. It is not unusual to find that around 50% of IT development projects are of limited, or no, business value.

Many companies are, of course, moving away from this model or avoiding it altogether. Barclays are well known for their setting up of Barclays Computer Operations as a quasi business, in order to introduce a more commercially minded culture into their systems department. One motor manufacturer is sensitising its IT operations to the commercial world, by linking its budget directly to the number of cars coming off the end of the production line—forcing IT management to challenge many of their own assumptions about how fixed their "fixed costs" are.

Other companies that are doing this, or similar moves, are also investing heavily in executive education so that business managers begin to understand their responsibilities in managing IT as a normal business resource. Too often, however, companies are "commercialising" or "customerising" their IT operations, without equipping their business managers with the means to take effective responsibility. It is still not unusual to find that an organisation views executive education on IT as an introduction to DOS, or even a beginner's guide to structured decomposition techniques.

The key lessons about the effect of the IT organisation on innovative/redesign projects are therefore:

- IT organisations can deaden innovation by forcing it to fit into a central plan.

- IT organisations can pervert, undermine and divert innovation because of technical performance measures and a lack of business awareness.

- IT organisations can prevent innovation by locking away resources on unimportant activities or overcontrolling their availability.

- Just reorganising the IT department is not enough.

Driver 3—The People, Skills and Procedures for IT Delivery. There is a conservatism at the heart of many IT professionals' skillsets and attitudes. It is a conservatism institutionalised by an addiction to structured methodologies, many developed as recently as the mid 1980s, and an understandable desire to defend their craft in the onrushing face of change. To put it another way, methodologies have a habit of institutionalising the past and then forcing the future to fit in, i.e. the past acts as the present condition for the future.

It is important to remember how many IT people cut their teeth on accounting and related financial systems. Accounting systems are easy to automate. There are externally and statutorily defined rules that must be followed. The Finance department has tended to have plenty of people who are systematic, structured thinkers, capable of expressing their needs in conceptual terms. This makes developing specifications much easier. The problem is that IT professionals are now being called upon to help in innovative, open ended projects dealing with less concretely defined areas of the business, like customer service systems (and proper customer service systems are not meant to be simply rejigged transaction processing systems). In these sorts of projects, documentation and analysis will not of itself give all the answers—and there is little chance of getting, and little point in pursuing, a 100% specification. Imagination must re-emerge as a core IT skill.

Of course there are many examples of people applying new skills and techniques with dramatic effects. One major food company is thinking of applying the principle that software should be treated as a disposable commodity with a life of no more than a year. BZW were reported in *Banking Technology* last year as taking a maximum of one year to move ideas from conception to full institutional implementation in their dealing room.

One specific skill area that is often dangerously misapplied is that of information engineering. Good information engineering skills are of course important in designing the information infrastructure which underpins new business processes; too often, however, the techniques and needs of information engineering hijack the process engineering exercise. The consequence is that too much effort goes into thinking about how the new processes will work, rather than what the new processes should be.

The key lessons about the effect of the people, skills and procedures for IT delivery on innovative/redesign projects are therefore:

- Innovation can be killed by overstructured, inflexible techniques designed for automating readily specifiable areas of business, such as finance.

- Process design can be hijacked too early and turned into an information engineering exercise.

Driver 4—The Existing Corporate Investment in Systems. In many ways this will decide how capable an organisation is at exploiting IT for business advantage. If IT has always been seen as a normal part of business operations and a vehicle for supporting and delivering business innovation and change then the omens are good, particularly if IT has been delivered to support cross-functional working with a customer focus. If IT has been a specialist preserve seen, at best, as a necessary evil serving a specific functional unit, then the chances are that neither the business nor IT operations are sufficiently skilled to exploit the potential of process based computerisation.

The key lesson about the effect of the existing corporate investment in systems on innovative/redesign projects is therefore:

- Much of the existing IT investment will have been functionally specific and the organisation will not be experienced in managing the complexities of cross-functional developments.

SUCCESSFUL INNOVATION WITH IT

Successful innovation with IT comes from keeping an eye on the ball of business change and business benefits, while avoiding being seduced into thinking that technology is the key issue and so something that can be left up to the IT department.

Most innovations start off with a good business idea, but then get hijacked into "systems development projects". Yet systems by themselves usually deliver nothing but cost. Business managers need continuously to remind themselves that business benefits from IT only accrue when people actually do something physically or mentally different with the system that is delivered—and this means actively managing to operationalise new ways of working.

In practical terms, Dr Lockett's study into 30 projects at a major multinational drew out six very specific recommendations for getting business success with IT projects:

- Ensure that there is a business champion for the project
- Establish a cross-functional team
- Limit technology risk
- Use prototyping
- Move from loose to tight management
- Market the new way of working like a new product

1. *Ensure that there is a business champion for the project.* In cross-functional, customer focused innovation this means ensuring that there is a business champion with sufficient standing to handle the inevitable turf wars that will erupt, as traditional functional boundaries are challenged or eroded. Whether it is a cross-functional or functionally based project, however, without a business champion in place to be responsible for the measurable benefits, a project will probably fail—and by champion this does not mean a passive, one day a month person, but someone willing to put in around 1 to 2 days a week where necessary.

2. *Establish a cross-functional team.* Cross-functional teams ensure that the wider perspectives of a project are taken into consideration, so that the needs and concerns of up- and down-stream departments are built into any new design. By pulling together this wide selection of people, not only is the cross-fertilisation of ideas facilitated but the message of mutual dependency is reinforced. During a process redesign exercise this is particularly important, since such a project is by definition cross-functional and therefore must not be hijacked by any one department. It will also allow fundamental, common design principles to be identified such as "don't accept rubbish and don't pass it on".

3. *Limit technology risk.* The old cliché still holds good—the leading edge

is too often the "bleeding edge" when it comes to using IT. Given the maturity of so many innovative computer technologies, however, there is hardly ever any excuse for not using proven IT. Given the political and organisational risks of process redesign, adding unnecessary technical risks to the equation is a sign of a very brave, or foolhardy, management team.

4. *Use prototyping.* Play! Experiment! Don't expect answers and solutions to arrive fully formed like Venus from the waves. Systems readily allow alternative scenarios to be played out or simulated. Beware, though, of falling in love with computer simulations when real life validation is often the best, or only, way of confirming assumptions.

5. *Move from loose to tight management.* Know when to play. Know when to stop. Many people are worried about missing a trick by stopping playing too early (or by not carrying out enough up-front analysis) but the point to bear in mind is that the final design will not be perfect, indeed cannot be perfect. The design you come up with is inevitably going to be a staging post towards another redesign—to criticise people for not perfecting an innovative design is like criticising the Wright Brothers for not coming up with the 747.

6. *Market the new way of working like a new product.* A new system and a new way of working needs to be sold—particularly when that new system and work process undermine many basic assumptions about how an organisation should work. New ways of working mean a change to the status quo and so an organisation will need to believe in both its head and its heart that changing the status quo is worthwhile. Accept that there will be an emotional attachment to the past and that this needs to be worked with, rather than ignored, when selling the new.

CONCLUSION

Process redesign is a form of innovation with a focus on the customer and consequently on cross-functional co-ordination. When a company embarks on rethinking how it can do business with these principles it is going to come across some "interesting" challenges when it comes to integrating IT into its thinking.

These challenges reflect the limitless potential of technology and its ability to rewrite the rules of corporate space and time, a lack of experience in cross-functional developments, a technical rather than business bias towards IT and a tendency for all projects involving IT to lose their business focus and turn into something called merely "technology projects".

REFERENCES AND FURTHER READING

S. Zuboff In The Age of the Smart Machine (Heinemann 1989)
M. Lockett "What Makes IT Work?" (Published in "Information Management: The Organisational Dimension" OUP 1992).
M. Walton The Deming Management Method (Mercury 1989)
C. Handy Understanding Organisations—Fourth Edition (for comments on Taylor et al) (Penguin 1993)
R. Walker Rank Xerox—Management Revolution (Long Range Planning Vol 25, No 1 1992)
C. Davidson Banking Technology June 1992, "Dealing with Speed Freaks"

3

Business Process Re-Engineering: Who Does What to Whom?

Chris L. F. Haynes

ABSTRACT

Business Process Re-Engineering is an activity undertaken on the line operations of an organisation. Three different groups—business strategists, quality process specialists and information systems providers—all have interests in helping line managements improve the way they discuss and detail the re-engineering activity. This is an obvious application for tools similar to the CASE tools used for specifying and designing the information components of the business process, but there is a severe danger—if this is done without careful analysis of the requirements of organisational dynamics—of applying inappropriate information-oriented models to the essentially human activity of change management.

Software Assistance for Business Re-engineering. Edited by Kathy Spurr, Paul Layzell, Leslie Jennison and Neil Richards
© 1993 John Wiley & Sons Ltd

ORIGINS OF BUSINESS PROCESS RE-ENGINEERING

The Information Systems community faces a new challenge in business process re-engineering (BPR): helping line managers improve what is already working. This doesn't sound difficult, but there is a significant shift in the kind of work we do and hence in the processes and tools we need.

In the early years of computing our basic approach usually assumed that we were 'automating' an **existing** clerical system. Thus many of the methodologies we have been using assume that our job is that of the detective, the anthropologist or the train-spotter. The 'process' which needed automating was already in existence as a clerical activity; we could go out and capture data, record activities, reproduce existing paper-based forms in an electronic medium and mimic well-established human work steps in COBOL code.

At a higher conceptual level, the organisation's data was already there to be inspected and was static in its definition. We could thus still have a reasonable expectation of being able to build enterprise-wide data models and even impose the discipline of the corporate data dictionary.

What many corporations ended up with in the 1980s was an organisation using the structures and processes that they developed in the 1930s when work practices had to be based around functional specialisation and clerical message-passing, but with inflexible and unmaintainable computer programs taking the place of flexible and adaptive humans.

COMPOSITION OF BPR

Business process re-engineering is a movement to fundamentally reassess these very structures and processes. It says to the Chief Executive Officer: 'Stop simply automating the old ways of working; see if, with new cultures, new business pressures and with new IT, there is a fundamentally better way of defining, organising and running your business'.

The first effect of this is to bring into **conscious discussion** the systems and processes of the current organisation. Surprisingly, this is not at all easy to do—general management lacks a common language for describing an organisation in all its dimensions; too often the simple tree structure diagram of who-reports-to-who is the only model managers know how to use. We, using the Information Sciences, offer only a very mechanistic, 'Taylorist' language of data, entities, events, and procedures (Morgan 1986). This clearly does not in any way represent the roles for creativity, innovation, judgement or relationship management that a healthy organisation needs.

We had better realise that the IT community could easily become one of the major hindrances to business process re-engineering. It is our 'applications backlog' which adds massively to the delays and risks of making changes to how the organisation works, it is our demands for corporate data dictionaries which ask the organisation to freeze its terminology and the content of all of its communications, it is our Taylorist approach which encourages concentration on a reductionist, convergent attitude and which gives no linguistic space or value to the activities in which humans make an enterprise into a vibrant organisation.

Let us first examine some of the ingredients of business process re-engineering before we move on to consider how our analysis methodologies and CASE tools could become an aid, not a hindrance, to this vital business task.

The 'Management in the Nineties' program at the MIT Sloan School of Management (Scott Morton 1991) devised the Strategic Alignment Model, which identifies four key components of a business:

- Business Strategy,
- Organisation infrastructure and processes,
- Information Systems infrastructure and processes,
- Information technology strategy.

This simple model has many lessons for us. It reveals, for example, that all too often we confuse an IT strategy with an IS plan. Most importantly, for this present topic, it insists on the essential, pivotal role of line management in the business and explains how 'deriving the IT Strategy from the Business Strategy' is an inadequate and misguided activity and has led to many spectacular failures in implementing IT.

The *business strategy* topic describes how the organisation intends to behave in its environment. It describes the markets, services, products and commercial policies it must pursue. It also may redefine exactly what the business IS—which are the outputs, and what are the attributes of these outputs, which give value to its customers.

The *organisation infrastructure and processes* topic is the top-level design of how the organisation is to work to deliver these outputs with the required attributes. This is the area in which business process re-engineering takes place. An organisation can be described as having three interrelated dimensions:

- Structure and Accountability
- Systems and Processes
- People and Culture

Every organisational change involves these three dimensions; most problems in organisational change happen because the change was perceived to be in only one of these dimensions—and was managed thus, ignoring the need to recognise and manage the related changes in the other two dimensions. One that many of you will be familiar with is the new information system which fails because no one appreciated and managed the impact on accountability, autonomy, power, and so on amongst the 'users': the structural and cultural dimensions of this organisational change were overlooked or underrated.

Any change in any one of these dimensions is a change to the organisation as a whole and requires planned complementary changes in the other two dimensions. BPR is the managed change of all of these dimensions for a purpose which is derived from the business strategy of the organisation. It is a deliberate attempt to change how the organisation as a whole works, not just to improve the productivity of one of the components of the organisation. It is a fundamental re-engineering of what the organisation does and how it does it, of its role in its customers' value chains.

Several management consultancies seem to be claiming to have invented the term 'business process re-engineering' or close synonyms, but it can be no accident that the term seems to have emerged from those consultancies close to the MIT Sloan School in Boston, Massachusetts while the MIT90s study was under way. It is the insights and challenges revealed by the Strategic Alignment Model and similar work which demand that directed and informed organisational development be better managed as a precondition to making more effective use of IT in the 1990s.

We might expect that there is a common language for describing business processes—before and after re-engineering. I am not aware of any one approach achieving common recognition; the most common current approach seems to be that offered by the 'Quality Gurus'. The message of the 80s, which has been generally received, is that the key to quality improvement is sound process management. The most common model is one of the simplest, yet seems rich enough for many of these present activities. This model of a process stage is simply:

- Inputs
- Process Stage
- Outputs

It uses a catalogue of the kinds of inputs and outputs (physical resources, knowledge and skills, etc.) that need to be considered. Those organisations pursuing ISO 9000 quality registration use models such as this to describe all their internal processes.

Most of the process description for quality purposes seems to be based on clerical-style forms with word-processor support; references to other processes usually take the form of references to other documents.

The tragedy is that, so far as I am aware, no one has managed to derive a common approach to describing processes which satisfies the three users of such a process description, namely:

1. The organisational designers, undertaking BPR,
2. The line managers, undertaking quality-related process management,
3. The IS community, analysing the information systems components of the process.

Historically the functions of users (2) and (3) have mostly related to the description of existing, relatively static organisations and have been seen as essentially disconnected activities.

BPR is different because it is about substantial change—with all the associated needs for analysis, synthesis, innovation, prediction and communication. It also spans or even re-shapes existing functional and organisational boundaries, so that any attempt to discuss or describe the change becomes immediately a political and cultural intervention in the organisation and thus part of the change process itself.

THE VALUE-BASED APPROACH

The thrust of this paper is to examine whether, within the methodologies, models and tools we have developed for describing information systems, we have the seeds of a broader approach for supporting the integration of all three approaches—driven by the needs of BPR. To do this, we should obviously consider the requirements of the BPR activity.

BPR is a creative, engineering process in which synthesis, innovation and intuition play as large a role as analysis, detailing and rule-making. At the heart of any support for BPR must be a representation schema that gives business strategists and organisational designers the ability to describe the concepts and attributes by which they judge an organisation. They must then be able to manipulate and quantify possible alternative implementations of that organisation.

There does not appear to be any commonly-accepted methodology for BPR yet, but the results of the MIT90s program suggest that the core of the approach involves re-engineering the value chain from the points of customer contact inwards—deliberately avoiding the influence of any existing internal organisational assumptions.

There is an iterative approach which follows the following stages:

1. Consider the customer of a business activity: identify which attributes of the product (or service) have the highest values to him.

2. Consider what a new entrant to this market would have to do to deliver the product with these value-attributes maximised. Identify the three or four top-level processes which have the greatest impact on these attributes—which control the value to the customer—and note which properties of these processes most affect the customers' values.

3. Treat each of these key processes as a 'customer' for further internal sub-division of the work of the organisation or its suppliers. Treat the required properties as representing the 'value' for these intermediate customers.

4. Repeat the above three steps until the overall business activity has been sufficiently decomposed.

This approach will give a first top-down process design in which the higher levels of abstraction are most closely related to the value perceived by the customer, whereas most conventional organisational designs start immediately to split the organisation by traditional function and tend to give the greatest prominence to the largest functions, i.e. those which have the greatest cost.

It is very important to concentrate on value, not cost. Cost will 'come out in the wash' at the end of the process; too early a concentration on cost will probably cause an activity which is insignificant to the old organisation, but vital to the customer, to be overlooked or 'traded-out'. Using value, and considering two or more different market segments for the same business (by definition these different segments appreciate different values in the product offer) helps give BPR this 'edge' which makes it relevant to the customer, not to the organisation itself.

Suppose one were re-engineering a passenger air transport system in Europe. Business travellers probably give the highest value to the precision of the actual arrival time—they want to be able to arrive just in time for a meeting with a very low probability of being delayed. An airline organising to optimise the value it gives to these customers would probably make its relationships with the various Air Traffic Control authorities one of the first, most important, functions of their business, since it is the poor air traffic control process over Northern Europe which introduces the greatest variability in actual arrival time.

If the same airline were also to serve the needs of the packaged holiday traveller with small children it might perhaps decide that the factor that parents value the most is minimising the time for which children are constrained in aircraft or coach seats, away from play areas or toilet facilities. The actual time of arrival at the holiday hotel—within an hour or two—is of less importance for these travellers as long as any delays can be made 'part of the holiday' for the children and meals and rest breaks are provided when needed. For this market segment the airline might decide that having their own family-oriented departure lounges and very carefully managed passenger logistics (low fuss movement to the aircraft, no long in-aircraft waits for flight clearance, an arrival hall with rest facilities before a long onward coach journey) would be what these customers value.

Both of these markets needed the top level of the airline process to be concentrated on 'passenger care' aspects. The high cost activities of owning and maintaining the aircraft, in-flight catering and the back-office booking functions—which might in a conventional organisational design dominate the top-level functional design—have little direct value to the customer. The fact that there is an air-worthy plane waiting with its crew, and that the customer is able to buy a ticket and has a meal every few hours, is taken for granted—that's fundamental to being in that business and is not **valued** by customers.

This value-chain analysis might thus identify the air traffic control relations and the (closely-related) passenger logistic activities as the most important in the organisation. The BPR process would then proceed to break down these activities, again concentrating on those processes which most affect the values perceived by the customers.

REQUIREMENTS ON BPR METHODOLOGIES AND TOOLS

What will emerge from this process is a quite new perspective on how the organisation has to operate, and hence on its Information Systems needs.

What we must offer BPR are the methodologies and supporting languages and tools which:

1. Support this initial analysis of business process decomposition with a value-based orientation—enabling quantification of the possible alternative value chain arrangements,

2. Enable the new process designs to be described, discussed and documented at a stage where both human and IT activities are not yet distinguished and where numerical metrics and targets can be established,

3. Enable the information systems designs to be developed in harmony with the human aspects of the organisational design,

4. Enable a smooth transition from the existing to the new systems to be planned and implemented—without interrupting the business.

These four points identify the essential requirements for support for Business Process Re-engineering. The task we now have is to specify and construct the methodologies and tools which have these properties. That must be the subject of later papers.

REFERENCES

Morgan, G. 1986, *Images of Organisations*, Sage Publications
Scott Morton, M. S. 1991, *The Corporation of the 1990s*, Oxford University Press

Section 2

Does It Help to Have Methods and Tools for Business Re-Engineering?

Paul Layzell, Leslie Jennison

> *Though this be madness, yet there is method in it.*
> Hamlet Act II, Scene 2, W. Shakespeare

A black art, or a scientific method? In recognising the need to redesign a business or set of business processes, the immediate question is *how to do it?* It may be argued that the diversity of factors which influence the success or failure of a business makes any methodical or systematic approach to business re-engineering misguided and inappropriate. Traditionally products, processes and procedures have been comprehensively described using a variety of techniques, many drawn from the IT community. But less tangible factors also influence the performance of a business: economic, sociological, organisational and psychological. These factors impinge upon issues such as customer satisfaction, customer loyalty, the degree and acceptability of change.

Software Assistance for Business Re-engineering. Edited by Kathy Spurr, Paul Layzell, Leslie Jennison and Neil Richards
© 1993 John Wiley & Sons Ltd

Following the general approach of business re-engineering itself, this book started with business requirements for re-engineering, and now continues with an examination of the process or method for achieving it. The next six papers focus on some detailed techniques, tool support and management, and show how some of the techniques and concepts have translated into software.

We start with an overview of how techniques may be integrated, take a tour of information gathering and process modelling, and end this section with the project management aspects of business re-engineering.

Julian Watts' paper *A Practical Approach to Redesigning and Implementing Business Processes* is written from an Information Engineering viewpoint. He describes the integrated framework for business re-engineering used by James Martin & Company. It draws on a *tool kit* of techniques, including value stream and quality management techniques, related to Information Engineering through shared concepts of business activity, data, and the interaction between them. Information Engineering has always encouraged close links between business strategy and information system development. The relationship between business re-engineering and software engineering is important because, as Julian Watts and several other contributors observe, information systems are a vital component of many re-engineered processes. Understanding the relationship helps the business engineer and the information engineer to achieve the rapid implementation of a redesigned process. The alignment of common concepts and deliverables has assisted tool constructors and tool users in exchanging information between business re-engineering tools and CASE tools.

Gary Born's paper *Apache: A Pictorial CASE Tool for Business Process Engineering* is based on practical experience at EDS-Scicon, and addresses initial data collection and analysis of existing processes using the Apache tool. Apache's strength lies in its ability to capture process knowledge at the level of an individual perspective and a pictorial representation of a process. The tool is used within an overall approach of understanding business goals and processes, analysis of existing processes, process redesign, and finally the transfer of revised business models to a systems development environment. The effectiveness of such a tool is impressive: in one study it identified *processing which was unknowingly repeated five separate times*. This demonstrates what can be achieved by deployment of consistency checking, path analysis and data definition tools. These more mundane aids are just as important as the most glamorous graphical process diagram.

Tim Huckvale and Martyn Ould in their paper *Process Modelling: Why, What and How*, also recognise that process modelling is the key to successful business redesign. They address key issues in the modelling activity, such as handling complexity, and knowing when a model is complete enough for the purpose. But business re-engineering is not just another form of system development activity: traditional DP modelling techniques, with their emphasis on data, are not good at capturing the key elements of interest in modelling business processes. Drawing on their own experience at Praxis, embodied in the STRIM method, they promote a behavioural and organisational approach. The key concepts of business goals, rules, activities and interactions form the basis of business process modelling. Role Activity Diagrams are used to integrate these elements in a description of the interpersonal communication which is so essential to understanding business processes. The resulting model is a basis for quantitative analysis and process redesign.

The use of quantitative tools for *learning* about relationships between process structure and process performance is pursued in the next paper. Richard Stevenson, in *Strategic Business Process Engineering: a Systems Thinking Approach Using* ithink argues that a process engineering tool should be understandable and usable by managers. ithink is a graphical simulation tool with a world view based in system dynamics, aimed at the design activities of business re-engineering. Its forte is to provide a systemic and dynamic perspective of process behaviour and performance. The benefit of using simulation and prototyping tools lies in rapid testing of the business engineer's creative ideas. Richard Stevenson rightly emphasises that simulation can make process design *an intensive learning experience*. A good tool allows the exploration of many ideas as well as providing testable criteria for selecting the most promising solutions. The Health Service example is well worth following. Modelling showed how the behaviour of system components can produce a result which is the opposite of the objectives of the system as a whole. This can be a salutary lesson for the business engineer, and an excellent example of the role of the intelligent use of tools.

Just as in Richard Stevenson's description of **ithink**, a simple but powerful set of concepts underpins the prototype simulation tool, CADDIE. Faramarz Farhoodi's paper, *CADDIE: an Advanced Tool for Organisational Design and Process Modelling*, gives us a glimpse of how distributed Artificial Intelligence, Object Oriented programming and organisational theory are being combined by Logica in the construction of a research tool for consultancy support. The agent concept is especially interesting because an agent has knowledge, not only of how to perform tasks, but also about itself, its environment, and about events. Faramarz Farhoodi shows the behavioural and diagnostic power that can be achieved by modelling this local level of knowledge. He describes an Emergency

Services scenario which simulates the behaviour of organisations and individuals. As the scenario unfolds, each agent acts on the basis of local knowledge, and so can be interrogated to deliver insights into why individual behaviour occurs. This paper may look a little technical in places, but many business engineers will, as they design processes, benefit from the insight offered by Logica's approach. This type of modelling offers great diagnostic potential in analysing how the execution of a process may fail to achieve an operational goal.

The final paper in this section, *The Development Environment for Business Process Re-engineering* from Chris Moss at Softlab, addresses the issues of managing a re-engineering project and the general strategy and method to be employed. In this paper, environment is defined as the set of people carrying out, and the activities and tools used during the project. Since a business re-engineering project is always conducted within some framework or environment (whether it is explicitly designed or implicitly assumed), it is important to recognise and understand this environment. Chris Moss suggests that the environment for business re-engineering is characterised by three components: the human issues to be addressed, the activities to be performed, and the supporting tool set. The paper provides a comprehensive list of the factors to be considered within each of these components, and is a useful starting point for any manager about to embark on a business process re-engineering project.

Do methods help business redesign? Is there method in the madness? These papers demonstrate that there are many different perspectives on the method issue. Some might argue that the level of analysis is too detailed in some of the approaches described in these papers, and that it is easy to lose sight of the higher level issues and goals of trying to understand the broader scope of the business. However, the techniques have been applied in practice with significant impact on business redesign. By addressing the variety of management issues which need to be considered, Chris Moss attempts to put these methods in some perspective.

We are at an interesting and exciting stage in the evolution of tools to support business re-engineering. Some of the best ideas from different disciplines (such as organisational behaviour, business management, process control) mentioned in these papers are appearing, in different combinations, in the tools that are now becoming available. Earlier tools used for business re-engineering were often borrowed from these disciplines or from general purpose modelling, calculation, or information systems modelling. Current tools show signs of having learnt from the limitations of applying tools and techniques that address only some aspects of the problem. As Julian Watts and Chris Moss point out, tools also need to communicate with each other. There is a good chance that market pressures and a wider understanding and convergence of the underlying concepts will encourage this interaction. This will offer the business engineer a variety of sources of knowledge about a process, and provide mechanisms for exploiting the process design more directly in the construction of new procedures and information systems to support the process.

There remains one front on which tools can probably make little advance. Tools are splendid aids to modelling and design, but are no substitute for human creativity and ingenuity; they will therefore remain an aid, but not a substitute, for human business process engineers and process managers.

Section 4 of this book contains overviews of the tools described in these papers and others that were demonstrated at the Business Process Engineering Seminar. There you will find contact points for further information about the tools. We hope that you may enjoy using some of the techniques and tools described in this book, and that they will assist and enrich your practice of business re-engineering.

4

A Practical Approach to Redesigning and Implementing Business Processes

Julian Watts

ABSTRACT

While there are many issues involved in Business Process Engineering (BPE), this paper focuses on two of the most common practical problems which must be overcome to implement BPE successfully. The first problem is the integration of BPE with other initiatives such as business strategy, quality approaches and IT development methods. The second problem involves turning a theoretical redesign into a working process which delivers business benefit. This paper describes how some organisations have dealt with these problems on their way to improving performance through business process engineering.

Software Assistance for Business Re-engineering. Edited by Kathy Spurr, Paul Layzell, Leslie Jennison and Neil Richards
© 1993 John Wiley & Sons Ltd

INTRODUCTION

A new epidemic is currently sweeping through organisations in the UK. The symptoms include high levels of fatigue, raging cynicism and debilitating confusion. The cause of the epidemic is a disease known as "initiative overload" which has a particularly virulent strain called "business process redesign". The disease is caught through coming into contact with "hype" and sufferers endure repetitive strain injuries from hearing endless recitals of success stories such as "Ford" and "Mutual Benefit Life". No antidote yet exists but a vaccine has been developed which combines with the positive aspects of the virus to strengthen the corporate body. The vaccine is administered as a three-part solution containing coordination, pragmatism and results. Patients receiving the vaccine usually experience significant improvement in their health from their pre-epidemic days.

Most organisations suffer from initiative overload—the seemingly endless and random introduction of performance improving approaches. Executive management can see the benefit of each individual initiative, but often feel genuine frustration at the inability to set each initiative in context and communicate this effectively to the organisation. Each initiative usually gains some enthusiastic supporters as the concepts, theories and benefits of the new approach are discussed. However, once the approach moves beyond the theoretical stage towards practical implementation, uncertainty increases and the initiative gradually fizzles out, thereby setting the scene for the cycle to be started once again with the next new initiative. The organisation becomes increasingly cynical about the next flavour of the month and more resistant to change.

It would be easy to dismiss Business Process Engineering (BPE) as the latest fad but this would deprive the organisation of the opportunity to benefit from the types of major performance improvements experienced by other organisations. However it is clear that the complexity of process engineering means that it is difficult to implement BPE successfully. This paper attempts to address two of the major practical concerns surrounding BPE—how does BPE fit with other initiatives and how can a (theoretical) redesign be implemented in a pragmatic way? The paper describes a framework which sets a number of common initiatives in context and then focuses on how two initiatives—BPE and the Information Engineering Methodology (IEM)—can be closely integrated to enable the rapid introduction of high quality redesigned business processes.

INTEGRATING BPE WITH OTHER INITIATIVES

A framework that has been used successfully by a number of organisations shows how the organisation's vision of change can be brought about through a combination of radical change, continuous change and leveraging business change through IT (Figure 1). The vision provides the context for the other three change processes. It outlines where the organisation wants to be in the future and the extent to which it must change to achieve the vision. To achieve the vision, the organisation will probably need a combination of the other three change processes. Radical business change involves fundamental changes in the way the business views its customers and how it seeks to meet those customers' needs. Performance improvements of around 80% are necessary to achieve the step change required. Continuous change focuses on an aspect of the business and seeks to improve performance through the ongoing introduction of relatively minor enhancements. While each enhancement may result in performance improvements of only 1-5% the cumulative result over time is significant and means that competitors always have to be moving just to keep up with the organisation. Continuous incremental improvements complement the more radical step change—once a redesigned process has been introduced it can be continually improved until it requires another radical change in the future (Figure 2).

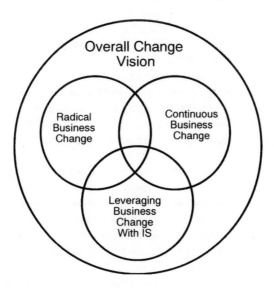

Figure 1   Integrate enterprise change

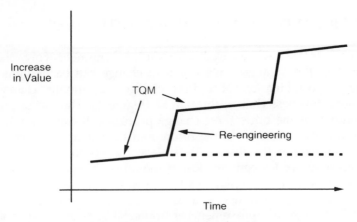

Figure 2   Continuous improvement and "breakthrough"

Information technology (IT) can be an input to the change process by highlighting opportunities for new products or markets, new ways of reaching the customer or better ways of working. Technology is an important contributor, but not the only source of ideas, for radical change. However, rather than focus on how IT can help to generate radical ideas (a major subject in its own right), this paper concentrates on how to deliver the information systems necessary to support the redesigned process.

A toolkit of approaches to support each of the four change processes has been developed by James Martin & Co. These toolkits are Strategic Visioning, Business Re-engineering, Quality Management and Information Engineering (Figure 3).

Strategic Visioning outlines the desired future state of the organisation—what it should be doing, how it will work and what will motivate it to achieve the vision. The future state is compared to the current realities and a set of principles are developed which will enable the organisation to close the gap between the current and future states, thereby achieving the vision.

Business Re-Engineering (BRE) involves the fundamental analysis and radical redesign of business processes, social systems, organisational structure and management approaches to achieve the required dramatic performance improvements in customer satisfaction, quality, costs or speed outlined in the vision. The process can extend across the whole organisation as the process starts with a customer need or request and ends when the need is satisfied.

Once the business process has been radically redesigned, quality management approaches can be used to fine-tune activities within

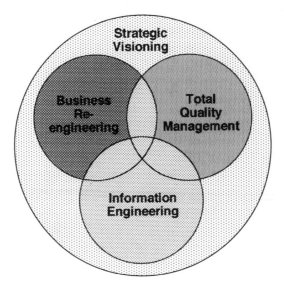

Figure 3   Four integrated change "toolkits"

the process. All employees are involved in the continuous search for opportunities to improve the processes in which they are involved. Employee creativity is complemented by statistical analysis to identify problem areas.

The Information Engineering Methodology (IEM) provides an integrated set of tasks and techniques to deliver high quality information systems which support the redesigned business processes and facilitate their ongoing improvement. It enables the business to prioritise development projects in line with business objectives and supports the co-ordination of development activities.

All the change processes share an interest in what the business wants to do (processes) and what it needs to know in order to do it (information). Strategic visioning provides an artist's impression of what the organisation should be doing in the future. BRE questions why a process is carried out and why the information is needed. Quality management looks for ways to make the output of an activity (which usually includes information) more useful for the recipient. IEM focuses on automating the required process in the most effective way to meet the information needs of those involved in the process. The key is understanding the required processes and information—this enables the various initiatives to be integrated and managed in a practical manner. Figure 4 shows how the required processes and information can be represented as diagrams known as the information

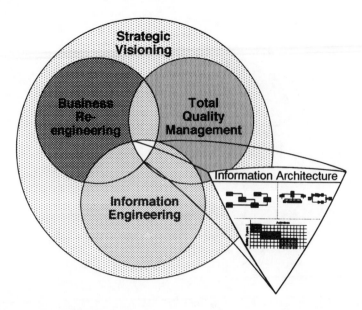

Figure 4   Enterprise engineering

architecture. The information architecture is merely a pictorial view of what the business wants to do and what it needs to know about. However, it is useful as it moves the conceptual framework outlined above on to a practical level where pragmatic decisions can be made about the co-ordination and integration of the various initiatives. For example, the architecture can provide details of the current process and information at the start of a business re-engineering project. Once the process has been redesigned the new process is fed back into the architecture along with any new or amended information requirements. Systems development projects are then identified and scoped to deliver the new process. Activities can be flagged as being under review by quality management and any changes made can be reflected back into the architecture models and subsequently reflected as changes to information systems.

The framework outlined in Figure 3 attempts to help executives identify how initiatives such as Strategic Visioning, Business Re-engineering, Quality Management and Information Engineering can fit together. The information architecture (Figure 4) is an approach which enables the integration of these initiatives to be planned and managed at a very practical level. The rest of this paper focuses on how two of the initiatives—business re-engineering and IEM—can be further integrated to enable the rapid implementation of redesigned business processes.

BUSINESS RE-ENGINEERING

Value streams—the key re-engineering concept

Before launching into the main tasks within the re-engineering approach, it is worth describing one of the key concepts used in business re-engineering—the value stream. When asked to describe what their organisation does, most people think in terms of the organisational structure or produce an activity hierarchy which usually resembles the organisational structure fairly closely. The focus is usually inward looking. Figure 5 represents this functional or hierarchical view by the vertical bars. The value stream takes the customer's perspective. It puts itself in the customer's shoes and asks "what gets done to meet my (the customer's) needs?". The value stream usually cuts across a number of divisions (and possibly organisations) and is represented by the horizontal bar in the diagram. For example, meeting the customer's need for a product might involve a number of departments including sales, credit checking, stores and distribution. Figure 6 illustrates this cross-functional view. The value stream therefore starts and ends with the customer and contains the cross-functional set of activities carried out to meet the customer's need. The term customer is used here to mean any person or organisation, both internal or external, which has a need that the business attempts to satisfy. For example, a business unit is an internal customer which needs staff, money and equipment. Each one of these needs is satisfied by a set of activities usually involving a number of departments. Other external customers might include regulators, the media, or the local community, each of which has their own needs which the organisation attempts to satisfy.

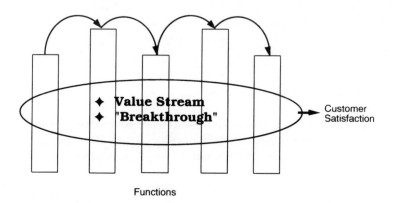

Functions

Figure 5   Value stream

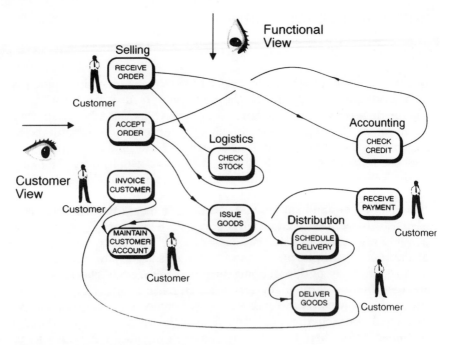

Figure 6 Value stream—functional view

While it is useful to identify all the various customer types and the value streams which meet their needs, it is important to recognise that the key customers are those that actually buy the organisation's products or services. It is critical to the business that the value streams that meet the buying customer's needs deliver satisfaction to these customers. In organisations where the activities within the value stream have evolved over a long period of time, it is likely that redesigning the value stream will deliver both large gains in customer satisfaction and reductions in cost.

The main stages of business re-engineering

Having described one of the key re-engineering concepts, it is easier to describe how value streams can be used to redesign business processes. The main stages of BRE are shown in Figure 7 and outlined below.

- *Position and plan BRE* identifies candidate areas for significant improvement. It provides the framework to ensure a common understanding of and agreement on the desired results of the project.

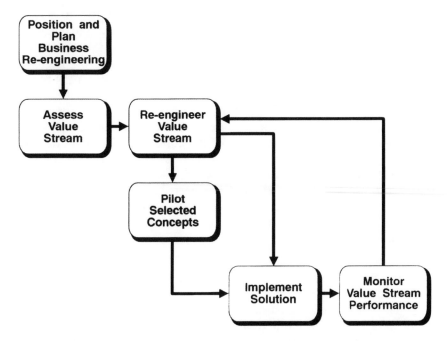

Figure 7 Business re-engineering: major tasks

The end results of the positioning phase of the project include committed management, a trained team and an identified value stream to be re-engineered. The key factor in BRE projects, given their radical, cross-functional nature, is business executive commitment. The activities carried out within the positioning phase should therefore vary depending on the level of agreement about the BRE project. For example, in situations where most of the executive is sceptical about BRE, it is useful to quickly identify and assess some broken processes to demonstrate the potential for improvement. Where scepticism verges on antagonism, it is likely that the project will fail. In this situation it is important to establish a shared vision through Strategic Visioning before attempting any BRE projects. Where there is broad based support for the project, the team should proceed as quickly as possible to deliver benefits which reinforce people's commitment. The key is to be sensitive to the political and social aspects of the individual organisation and select the appropriate approach to building agreement.

- The primary purpose of *Assess value stream* is to determine how well the business process is currently carried out.

The starting point is to identify the customers and their underlying needs which the organisation is trying to meet. By talking to customers these needs and the way in which the needs are satisfied can be identified. The activities currently carried out to meet the needs are identified and an assessment is made of the contribution of each activity to the customer satisfiers. The activities are also analysed to identify time, costs, problems, resources, responsibilities and other appropriate measures. The relative performance of other organisations is also analysed. Once the performance of the current value stream has been assessed, it is possible to determine if there is a valid cost/benefit case for re-engineering the process and its priority compared to re-engineering other processes. If a re-engineering exercise is required, outrageous goals can be set for the re-engineering team based on an understanding of the current performance, the vision and the performance of other organisations.

- *Re-engineer value stream* generates ideas which will significantly improve business performance, assesses their impact and determines how to implement the changes.

In order to reach the outrageous goals set for the re-engineering team, creative thinking is required to unearth radical ideas. There are a number of techniques which help people think creatively, including briefings on new technology. However, most radical ideas seem to emerge from focusing on the customer needs and the key principles on which the redesign should be based rather than the technology. Once the most promising ideas have been selected from all those generated, each idea or redesign option is developed in more detail. The new set of activities required by the option is identified. Just as the current activities were assessed for their contribution to customer satisfiers, and analysed in terms of costs, time, responsibilities etc., so each redesign option is also assessed using the same measures. It is extremely unlikely that each option will be perfect first time, so each redesign option cycles through design, analysis and further design. When each option is fairly well refined in terms of its contribution to customer satisfaction, the impacts on the cultural, organisational and political aspects of the organisation are assessed and further amendments carried out as appropriate. When the options are relatively stable, the most appropriate redesign option is selected and plans are developed for piloting and implementation.

- *Pilot selected concepts* tests whether the radical changes will work for the enterprise.

Because of the radical way in which re-engineering changes the organisation and its relationship with the customer, it is usually sensible to test out the selected redesign before rolling it out across the business. All the elements of the re-engineered process, including new activities, organisation structures, roles, and reward, control and information systems should be piloted. This transition from theoretical redesign to implemented process usually highlights the need for further refinement of the re-engineered process.

Piloting and redesigning the process are complementary and it can be helpful to build small scale prototypes of some of the options during the previous phase to help in the selection process.

- *Implement solution* prepares the organisation for change and rolls out the redesigned process.

Once the lessons learned from the pilot project have been incorporated into the redesign, the new process can be rolled out to the rest of the organisation. Depending on the value stream and the scale of the implementation, this could take from a few months to a few years. Two key factors in ensuring that the re-engineered process is implemented successfully are excellent planning and cultural change management. The implementation of a new process can be extremely complex, involving the introduction of new technology, organisation structures and roles. It is essential that thorough project planning and management is carried out throughout the implementation. One of the main reasons why re-engineering projects fail is the lack of attention paid to cultural and social aspects of the process. The implementation plan should include a change management programme to address people's underlying concerns, values and beliefs about the new process. It is relatively easy to come up with an excellent theoretical redesign, which increases customer satisfaction while reducing costs, only to find it is watered down or ignored by the people involved in delivering the process.

- *Monitor value stream performance* evaluates the new implemented process against the outrageous goals originally set for the redesign.

Once the new process has been implemented, the organisation has a further opportunity to learn about the process of re-engineering business processes. By monitoring the performance of the new process, the organisation can assess how well it achieved the outrageous goals initially set for the project and the accuracy of performance improvements suggested by the pilot. The ongoing monitoring of performance enables the use of continuous quality improvement approaches to refine the new process.

The opportunity for the organisation to learn about its ability to re-engineer processes should not be left exclusively to the last phase, but should be carried out throughout the re-engineering project. This enables the re-engineering lessons learned to be fed into other BRE projects as soon as possible.

The stages of BRE outlined above represent an approach based on the experience of assisting a number of organisations with business re-engineering. It is a toolkit from which people can select the activities and techniques that will be most appropriate for re-engineering their own organisation.

But so what? Does business re-engineering actually work and what business benefits have been achieved through re-engineering business processes? Rather than quote someone else's well known and distant experiences in the US, it may be more useful to consider more local projects in which the author has been personally involved. The results of the projects ranged from significant to radical improvements in performance, and as always, with the benefit of hindsight and experience, even more could have been achieved.

For example, a project to automate the existing credit customer engagement process for a high street retailer of white goods, was rescoped to start with a business redesign exercise. The new process involved devolving responsibility for decision making to the retail outlets and changing the organisation structure. The redesign reduced the time to meet the customer's request by a third. Bad debts also reduced by a six-figure sum as retail staff, who had bypassed the old process because it took too long, became responsible for the new streamlined process. The new IT system supported the new process rather than automating the old.

A leading life assurance company tested the hype around BRE by carrying out a 'proof of concept' exercise. The new policy creation process involved parallel working, new roles and organisation structure, all supported by new IT systems. The time to set up the policy—a key factor in the competition for business from independent financial advisors—reduced from several weeks to several days, a performance improvement of around 80%.

Two other particularly interesting projects covered the purchasing and change management processes. In both these projects, the number of customer satisfiers met by the existing process was so low that the redesign actually increased the number of activities in order to fully satisfy the customer.

The conclusion, based on personal experience, is that business re-engineering does make a substantial difference to business performance. It is not the universal panacea, but organisations will deprive themselves of an opportunity to improve their performance if re-engineering is dismissed as the flavour of the month.

THE INFORMATION ENGINEERING METHODOLOGY (IEM)

Business re-engineering results in new business processes which often require the support of information systems. Organisations can avoid considerable pain and cost by using an approach to re-engineering which is integrated with methods for delivering information systems. Having described above an approach to re-engineering, this paper now briefly describes the Information Engineering Methodology—a business driven approach to delivering information systems. Finally, having described the approaches to both business re-engineering and systems development, this paper will continue by outlining how the two methods can be closely integrated to enable the rapid implementation of redesigned business processes.

As this paper has been prepared for a British Computer Society conference, it has been assumed that most readers are familiar with many of the techniques within IEM. The paper therefore concentrates on describing some of the principles of IEM and outlining the various paths through the methodology.

IEM—redesigning the systems delivery process

The most fruitful business processes to re-engineer are usually those which have developed in a piecemeal way over a number of years, have used technology to automate parts of the process in a non-integrated fashion and currently deliver low satisfaction to the customer. Using these criteria, the business process of delivering information systems is a prime candidate for business re-engineering in most UK organisations. In many companies, development methods have grown by adding in useful techniques here and there over 20–30 years. CASE tools have been brought in to automate different parts of the process and rarely support the full development process in an integrated manner. The number of business people delighted by the information systems which support them tends to be fairly low. The systems delivery process is therefore a prime candidate for business re-engineering and this is one reason why it is often difficult for the IT department to encourage the rest of the business to re-engineer the processes they carry out. The obvious and not unreasonable question for the business people to ask is "If business re-engineering is so good, why don't you apply it to the process you work on, before encouraging me to re-engineer the processes I work on?"

IEM has been described as an off-the-shelf redesign of the systems delivery process. The customers are the business people who rely on the systems and the customer satisfiers include systems characterised by the delivery of business requirements, reliability, flexibility and ease of use. As IEM is a redesign of the systems delivery process, the critical success factors identified above for BRE projects are very relevant. The successful implementation of IEM depends on excellent project planning and management, and attention to the change management issues. As a result, James Martin & Co. have developed the "Roadmap" approach to ensure the successful implementation of IEM (Figure 8). The Roadmap addresses all the project management, change management and technical issues necessary to ensure the new value stream of activities for systems delivery is tailored to the needs of the individual organisation and is implemented successfully.

IEM consists of an integrated set of activities, techniques, roles and deliverables which meet the customer's needs for information systems. The activities which make up the methodology reflect the key redesign principles necessary to ensure that the new systems delivery process meets the customer satisfiers. These principles are outlined briefly below. What the business wants to do and what it will need to know about is defined by business people facilitated by development staff. The organisation's requirements for information systems are therefore specified by business people, resulting in systems which deliver direct benefit to the business. This joint venture approach to systems development is a key principle of IEM and is supported by other principles which help business involvement. These include extensive use of diagrams, in-built iteration to refine requirements and a top-down approach which starts with the business strategy and progressively identifies more detailed business needs.

The value stream of activities in the IEM systems delivery process can vary depending on the type of system being developed. The alternative routes through the method are known as development paths and are shown in Figure 9. The main stages of the 'classic' Information Engineering path are:

- *Information Strategy Planning* which interprets the business strategy into information, systems and technology strategies and identifies the main areas of the business.

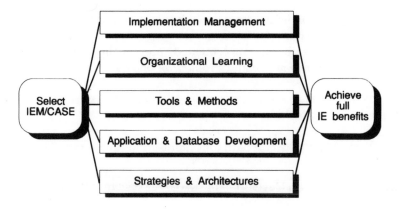

Figure 8 The Roadmap

Development Path	Planning	Analysis		Design			Construction
		Outline	Detailed	Outline	Detailed	Technical	
IE	ISP	Outline BAA	Detailed BAA	Business System Design	Technical Design		Construction
RAD		RP		User Design		Rapid Construction	
IE/RAD	ISP	Outline BAA		User Design		Rapid Construction	
Packages	ISP	Outline BAA	Package Selection and Implementation				
Reverse Engineering	ISP	Reverse Engineering					
Object Oriented	ISP	BAA w/ OO Extensions	Object Oriented Design & Construction				
Special Approaches	ISP	User Computing Knowledge Based Systems Development					
Structural	ISP	Technology Development Organizational Development					

Figure 9 Development paths

- *Business Area Analysis* focuses on one area of the business and identifies what the business wants to do and what it needs to know about to progressive levels of detail.

- The people who will use the system specify how it should look and feel, for example by defining what screens will be required, during the *Business Systems Design* phase.

- *Technical Design* defines how the technology will be used to deliver the information system.
- The system is built, implemented and maintained during the *Construction, Transition* and *Production* phases.

As well as the classic Information Engineering path, other paths through the methodology include:

- the Package Application path for organisations implementing software packages
- Rapid Application Development (RAD) for systems which are required within very short timescales
- the Client Server path for systems delivered on client server technology

The key is to select the path most appropriate to the needs of the business customers and the characteristics of the project.

The rapid growth in demand for CASE tools reflects the need for improvements in the process of delivering systems. Just as technology can generate radical ideas for business process redesign, so CASE tools as a technology have stimulated the search for improvements to the approach of delivering systems. However, while new tools and individual techniques on their own can provide incremental improvements in the systems delivery process, step change improvements can only be achieved through the radical redesign of the systems delivery process itself. For many organisations, IEM is a radical, off-the-shelf redesign of the systems delivery process which exploits the power of CASE tool technology and can be tailored to the needs of individual organisations.

DELIVERING SYSTEMS TO SUPPORT BUSINESS RE-ENGINEERING

The framework for integrating the change processes outlined at the start of this paper highlighted the role of business re-engineering and IEM. Both these change processes have been described in more detail in the preceding sections. The final part of this paper describes how business re-engineering and IEM can be integrated in a pragmatic manner.

BRE will remain an academic exercise for many organisations unless the redesigned business process is actually implemented. While it is dangerous to assume BRE always involves IT, the implementation of most redesign options usually involves some information systems to support the new process. It is clearly in the organisation's interest for the approach taken for BRE to be closely integrated with the approach used to develop information systems. Such integration enables the redesigned process to be implemented swiftly through the rapid introduction of new information systems. James Martin & Co.'s approach to BRE outlined above, has been developed to provide a seamless link between process redesign and implementation through IEM. This integration applies on two levels and is described below.

At one level, individual tasks and techniques from the IEM toolkit can be shared by the BRE toolkit. For example, the business requirements outlined in the redesigned value stream can be specified in more detail using common techniques. This helps the redesign team to clarify their thoughts on the redesigned process and systems development teams to identify the supporting technology required. Techniques from the IEM Business Area Analysis stage, such as data modelling and process dependency diagramming, can be pulled forward to help document the redesign options. These techniques describe what the business wants to do and what it needs to know about—areas which both the redesign team and the development team need to understand. By using the same techniques to understand the business, it is possible to provide the seamless integration of business re-engineering and systems delivery through IEM. Other techniques within the IEM toolkit are also useful in BRE projects. For example, the information systems used to support the current process can be documented following the "current systems analysis" task in IEM. This analysis is used in subsequent BRE stages to assess the impact of the various redesign options on the current systems and is a factor in developing the cost/benefit case of individual options.

The second level of integration involves the selection of the appropriate IEM path during the phases of the BRE project. IEM provides a number of paths to test or deliver the technology component of the new value stream in the redesign, pilot and implementation phases of BRE. For example, it may be appropriate to develop simple systems using the IEM Rapid Application Development (RAD) path to help decide which redesign option to select. Once an option has been selected, a working prototype could be developed again using the RAD path. The full implementation of the redesigned process may be delivered by following one of the other IEM paths, including the classic IEM, Package Application or Client Server paths.

It is possible to come up with a theoretical redesign of a business process by using a number of approaches. However, business re-engineering will remain an academic exercise unless the redesigned process is implemented effectively. One way to help ensure the effective implementation of the new process is to use an approach to business re-engineering which is closely integrated with a practical method for delivering the supporting information systems. The integration of Business Re-engineering and IEM enables the rapid introduction of high quality redesigned business processes.

CONCLUSION

A framework for integrating a number of initiatives was described at the beginning of this paper. Two of the initiatives—business re-engineering and IEM—were then described in more detail so that the practical means of integrating the redesign and implementation of business processes could be highlighted more easily.

BRE is clearly not the universal panacea which the hype surrounding it often suggests. Nor is the approach outlined above a secondary panacea for those disillusioned with the first. However, the author's experience is that BRE can result in dramatic improvements in an organisation's performance and that the approach described in this paper is a pragmatic solution for two of the key issues surrounding BRE—how does it fit with everything else and how do you deliver the redesigned process?

5

APACHE: A Pictorial CASE Tool for Business Process Engineering

Gary Born

ABSTRACT

Apache is a proprietary methodology and toolset that automates collection and automation of data for business process modelling and engineering. It also serves as a front-end to conventional CASE tools for systems analysis, design and later stages of the system life cycle. Apache is a product of the Antares Alliance Group, a software company jointly owned by EPS Inc. and Amdahl Inc.

This paper provides an introduction to Apache. It places the methodology in context with other EDS-Scicon approaches and tools for business modelling, from high-level strategic approaches to the detailed data capture and modelling which Apache handles. The software modules are described briefly.

The Apache methodology divides a study into four stages: Initiation, Interviews, Analysis and Transition. Each is described, along with the

Software Assistance for Business Re-engineering. Edited by Kathy Spurr, Paul Layzell,
Leslie Jennison and Neil Richards
© 1993 John Wiley & Sons Ltd

Apache tools which support it. The paper also illustrates the use of Apache for business process engineering and redesign and provides case studies as illustrations.

INTRODUCTION

It is interesting that the sudden explosion of interest in Business Process Engineering (BPE) coincides with a reawakening of interest in CASE tools and methods. On the face of it, one would expect them to be at odds, since BPE tends to reject the traditional approach to software specification and development and concentrate as much on engineering of human systems as on computer systems.

The fact remains that real-world systems are quite complicated, whether human or automated, and they require computer based tools to assist in representing, analysing and improving them. BPE is encouraging change in the paradigms used by CASE tools, but it cannot be efficient without them.

Existing CASE tools assist systems engineers in designing and implementing complex computer systems. However, few of them address the "front end" of the development lifecycle, with facilities to determine users' needs and, where necessary, the re-engineering and improvement of the systems which support human processes.

To assist in the study of business processes, EDS-Scicon has developed Apache, a methodology and associated software package that supports data collection and analysis. Information provided by an Apache study can be used to improve the current system or to create an entirely new computer system.

The Apache software package is an integrated suite of programs, running on the Macintosh family of personal computers. These programs perform one of two tasks, data collection or data analysis. Both tasks are facilitated by the use of a pictorial (or iconographic) representation of processes, which makes it easy to capture information directly into the computer during an interview and then to validate the representations and provide further information.

This paper provides an overview of Apache and its approach to Business Process Engineering. It describes the features of the Apache software and the Apache methodology. Finally it discusses the uses of Apache as a CASE tool and for analysis and re-engineering of business processes.

WHERE IS APACHE USED?

Levels of Modelling and Selection of an Approach

EDS-Scicon provides a comprehensive consultancy service, covering the entire enterprise and supporting systems and process management. In the specific area of Business Process Engineering (or Re-engineering), we recognise that there are various levels of modelling required, from strategic enterprise modelling to detailed process modelling. Apache is used mainly for the latter.

Apache has been used for business process modelling for a wide range of businesses and at varying levels of detail. However, it is most appropriate for detailed process modelling, where the processes are well-established and known by the participants in the process. It is also most appropriate when the data and information used by the processes are well-defined and can be described in some detail at the beginning of the modelling work.

While Apache can be used for other situations, such as capturing high-level processes, we generally apply other approaches. In the European Business Consulting Group, we have developed a technique for capturing processes at facilitated workshops, using movable colour-coded notes on plastic-laminated charts. The use of charts makes the processes visible and encourages discussion among the participants before the process descriptions are finalised. We then use widely-available process mapping tools to capture and draw these processes on the computer.

For strategic business modelling and information planning, we use a proprietary methodology called BIP (Figure 1). This is also supported by a software package, ADVANTAGE, which runs on both PCs and Macintosh computers.

The Apache Philosophy

When the emphasis is on a detailed capture of processes and information, we make use of the Apache methodology and toolset. Apache follows a bottom-up approach to gathering data, capturing in detail the business operations. In contrast to top-down facilitation and modelling, Apache is normally used in a one-to-one interview. At such a detailed level, where all the steps of a person's job are captured, it is more cost-effective, and usually more accurate, to work with individuals rather than with groups. Also, Apache's pictorial approach to process representation is ideally suited

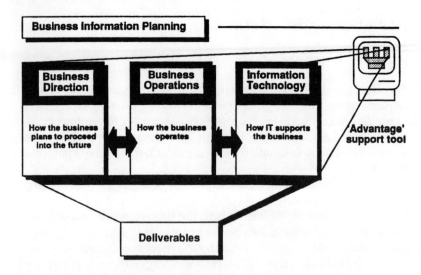

Figure 1   Business Information Planning and the Advantage Tool

for immediate discussion and verification with the person interviewed, speeding up the overall process of modelling.

THE APACHE CASE TOOL

Accurate, complete and consistent information is crucial to the success of all system analysis and design efforts. Understanding the current system is difficult for several reasons:

- Individuals have inaccurate or incomplete data.
- Information processing flow is highly complex.
- Managers and employees have different views of the same business functions.

The Apache approach is to identify—through interviews with process owners and other users—the people, information and processing that exist within the system.

Individuals are interviewed regarding their specific tasks and responsibilities. This information is captured electronically during the interview, ensuring accurate and consistent data collection and analysis.

Data Collection

Three Apache modules support data collection. **OrgChart** is used to create an employee database that allows the user to document the hierarchies of an organisation in an easy-to-read graphic format. **FormsEditor** is used to record information about each form or other discrete information item, within the scope of the study.

The main interviewing tool is the **Interviewer**. This application uses the data dictionaries produced by OrgChart and FormsEditor to document the processing and flow of information. The Interviewer application uses a pictorial representation to capture:

- Actions taken on information
- Justification of actions as some form of policy
- Decisions made based on the specific information provided
- Paths taken by information through an organisation

Besides providing an easily understood representation of the system (Figure 2), the icons ensure that only syntactically correct process descriptions are constructed.

The Apache interviewing technique is based on a bottom-up approach to gathering data, capturing in detail the business operations. The representation is event-driven, as non-IT staff usually find this the easiest way to describe the details of their job. Apache analysis tools can derive the data-flow representation of the processes by implication, from the event-driven processes which are recorded. The result is a flow diagram of the complete process (Figure 3). While partial aspects would have been captured in separate interviews, Apache is able to combine them to derive an overall view of the process.

Data Analysis

Apache provides several software modules for analysis of the data collected. The analysis tools provide:

- Error and reference reports
- Process flow (dataflow) diagrams
- Path and data flow analysis
- Data element definition
- Entity definition

70

Reservation clerk...Process Reservation Request

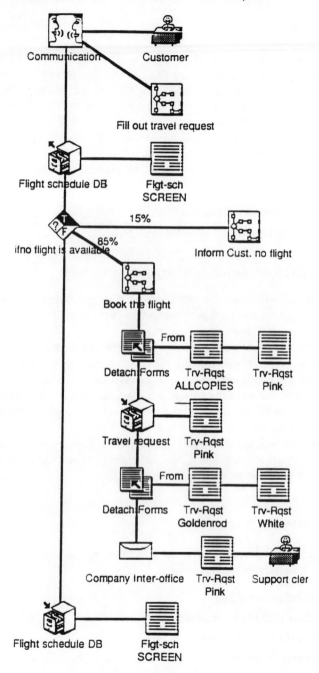

Figure 2 Apache's Pictorial Representation of a Process

Customer Order Process

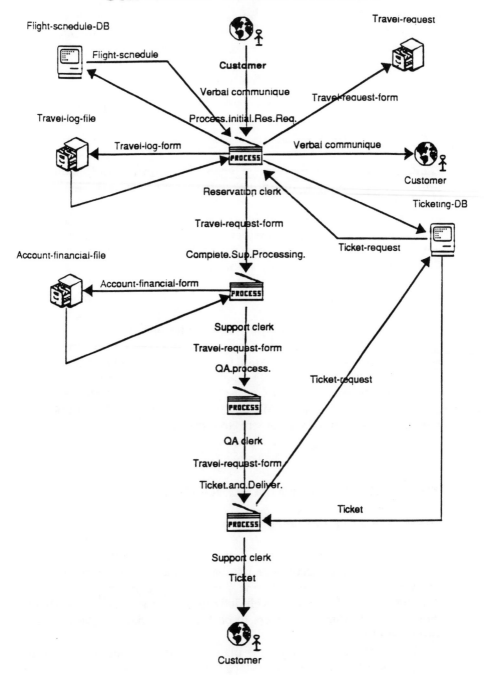

Figure 3 Apache Process Flow Diagram

ReportTool provides error and reference reports, which are used during data collection to tabulate and check the information being gathered. They also provide high-level management reports, including:

- Detailed descriptions of all job functions
- Details on the usage of each item of information
- Timing analysis information
- Process and data flow diagrams

GenCanvas is a drawing package, enabling the analyst to generate and improve the presentation of process flow diagrams, such as that in Figure 3.

Apache also supports path analysis and enumeration. Path analysis determines whether the networks derived from interviews are logically consistent. For example, it may identify a report which is produced but never used, or a file which is not consistently named by the interviewees. Path enumeration counts the number of paths from a source to a destination and provides a histogram of their frequency. This assists in re-engineering by suggesting areas of complexity in the current process definition.

Two final Apache modules provide both for analysis and for systems engineering. The Data Element Assignment Tool **DEAT** assists the user in assigning every item of information to a specific and unique data element. This enables the analyst to spot when information is copied, providing many opportunities for improvement through common databases.

The Entity Development Tool, **EDT**, is then used to identify entities and assign DEAT-defined data elements to those entities as attributes. Several screens are provided to assist the analyst—Figure 4 shows an example.

THE APACHE STUDY METHODOLOGY

Structure of an Apache Study

Within the Apache study team, duties and job functions are organised into several roles: project leader, database administrator, interviewer and analyst. For smaller studies, one person may perform several roles. Apache's ease of use and well-defined procedures enable relatively inexperienced system engineers to be trained quickly to take part in a system study.

We have also found that proper planning and preparation are essential to a successful study. Necessary steps include:

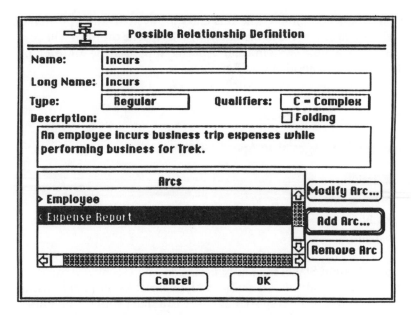

Figure 4   Example of the Entity Development Process with the EDT Module

- Determining the scope
- Defining job functions
- Creating data dictionaries
- Conducting preliminary interviews

For each job function, a person who performs that task is scheduled for an interview with a member of the study team. The interviewer brings a Macintosh portable computer with the employee and information data dictionaries and the Apache software. As the employee describes the actions he or she performs, the interviewer uses Apache to capture the details, as well as the initiating event(s) and timing information. Once an interview has been completed, the interviewer and interviewee will review and correct noticeable errors within the process chart. After completion of the review and clean-up, a textual language file is generated for use during analysis. Results from all interviewers are combined and analysed in regular sessions, which correct errors and resolve inconsistencies between different interviewers.

When all interviews are completed and error-free, analysis can continue and produce reports on the system to support the study's findings and recommendations. While this ends the system study portion of the development effort, the information which Apache captures will be useful in creating a new system, and Apache supports the transfer of this information into another CASE tool.

Stages in an Apache Study

There are four stages in an Apache study:

1. Initiation
2. Interviewing
3. Analysis
4. Transition

In the Initiation Stage, the study is scoped and essential Apache data is captured. Normally, that includes a hierarchical list of people within the study, who will be interviewed, and key external people or organisations. All relevant information is also identified and entered into the system with the FormsEditor application.

In the Interviewing Stage, people are interviewed individually. This stage also includes reconciliation of different interviews, to ensure that all information is named consistently and that the information provided is completely consistent. For example, one interviewee may state that he or she sends information to another person, but that other person might not mention receiving that information during their interview. The consistency checks will pick up this discrepancy and force the interviewers to obtain the correct information, before the study can continue.

After information from different interviews is fully reconciled and integrated, the Analysis stage evaluates the effectiveness of the current process and potential for improvements through re-engineering. The final stage, Transition, uses the DEAT and EDT tools to translate the results of Apache data into formats suitable for systems analysis and development.

APACHE AS A CASE TOOL

As noted above, Apache is a set of software tools for collecting data for process modelling and for analysis of the resulting process model. It is also a CASE tool and is used to model all aspects of the enterprise prior to development of new systems. Formerly we might have called this Requirements Analysis, but this normally was confined to analysis of the needs of a particular system. In common with other current holistic approaches, Apache views the possible system in the context of the whole enterprise, human as well as computer systems.

Apache is also integrated with INCASE, a CASE tool also produced by the Antares Alliance Group. If the results of an Apache study are to be used as part of the requirement or design of a new system, then Apache data is used as a starting point by feeding INCASE's repositories.

USING APACHE FOR BUSINESS PROCESS ENGINEERING AND RE-ENGINEERING

In the view of this paper, the focus of BPE (which sometimes is referred to by other names, including Business Process Re-engineering or Business Process Redesign) is documentation and redesign of the core and support processes of the enterprise; the systems or Information System component of this is only one of many. While computer, communications and other technological approaches are needed to *implement* solutions proposed by BPE, the focus of BPE itself is on much wider issues.

Consequently, to be useful as a tool for Business Process Engineering or Re-Engineering, software must assist the study team in analysing business processes and identifying areas where significant improvements are possible. Apache provides a large number of facilities for this. Some examples are shown below:

- Network analysis reveals areas of inefficiency and waste, including redundant information and processes, unused information and process repetition. It also determines cycle times, elapsed times and queuing times in a process. Figure 5 provides an example of a Process Timing Analysis with Apache. During re-engineering, Apache can be used to model the improved processes. By exporting the results of further Apache analysis, the before and after scenarios can be compared. Figure 6 shows an example of such a comparison, showing the elapsed time differences by functional areas.

- The "line item veto" assists in policy analysis. Using this feature, the analyst and the interviewee establish the proper set of policies and procedures for each process description. The underlying philosophy is that all procedures are to be supported by a policy, and that all policies lead to expressed corporate goals and objectives. Through an examination of the analysed processes, an Apache study assists

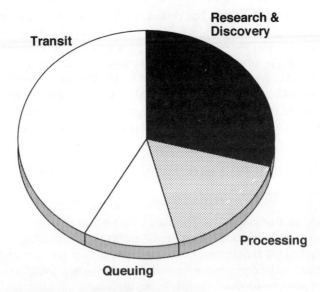

Figure 5   Example of Process Timing Analysis

management to determine how policies are implemented through the organisation and areas where their effectiveness can be improved.

- Path enumeration suggests areas of excess complexity. This provides an input to Business Process Re-Engineering, suggesting which areas are ripe for process simplification and streamlining.

- The DEAT and EDT tools can be used to reduce redundancy inherent in manual processes. In particular, they indicate processes where information is copied from one record to another. This is particularly useful where BPR utilises new computer systems, since the provision of shared information through common databases will make use of these results directly.

EXAMPLES OF APACHE STUDIES

Apache has been used as part of Business Process Engineering studies in a large number of areas, including:

- Expense report processing
- Vendor invoice processing

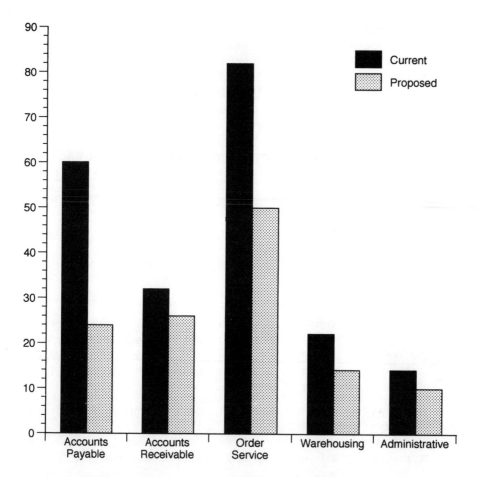

Figure 6   Apache Comparisons of Elapsed Time in a Process

- Fleet administration
- Time card accounting
- New customer account processing
- Corporate treasury operations
- Distribution business operations

The findings from these studies often have been startling. They include processing that was unknowingly repeated five separate times, field usage rates of only 50 percent and as many as four times the number of primary forms in the system than had been identified!

An example of a typical Apache study is provided by a study for a Customer Assistance Centre. The central problem was in response time: the centre was frequently missing the established target time for responding to and resolving a customer problem. The study was carried out over four months by a study team of six; 18 staff were interviewed and 340 items of information were registered for the study.

The three goals of the study were:

- Evaluate the processes supporting the handling of problem calls.
- Determine the reasons why the Centre was missing established cycle time targets.
- Recommend solutions that would enable the Centre to meet established targets.

The study provided 50 recommendations, each with the amount of time that could be saved by its implementation. Some of the key study results were:

- The study identified a lack of adequate staffing at peak customer calling periods and overstaffing during slower periods. Also, technicians did not have the experience or background to deal effectively with complicated customer needs. Rectifying these problems resulted in the average response time being reduced from 23 hours to a half-hour!
- As a by-product of the study, the Apache narratives derived from interviews were repackaged into Task Descriptions. As they were already in electronic format, they could be updated quickly, which reduced the cycle time to keep such documentation up to date.
- The study determined that technicians were required to enter data into up to five different computer systems. Identification and analysis revealed this problem and enabled the study team to define a simpler interface between systems. Requirements for new data input screens were defined. These changes resulted in greater cycle-time reductions and customer satisfaction.

CONCLUSION

Apache is a package of software which assists in acquiring and analysing information on business processes. It provides a pictorial language, enabling the interviewer to write a process description as the interview progresses, and then to validate the information immediately. It provides a full collection of analysis tools, including network analysis, policy analysis and consistency checking.

These analysis tools provide considerable support for Business Process Engineering. They can identify areas of inefficiency, waste and excess complexity. They can correlate goals with procedures and identify inconsistencies in applying policies. Apache also assists in the conversion from manual to automated systems, by identifying data which is duplicated and indicating where common databases would provide significant benefit.

6

Process Modelling: Why, What and How

Tim Huckvale, Martyn Ould

ABSTRACT

Business Process Engineers are interested in the way people work together to achieve business objectives. They need *process models* for describing, communicating, analysing and designing business processes.

Traditional DP modelling techniques, with their emphasis on *data*, are not good at capturing the key elements of interest in modelling business processes. This paper presents a view of what those key elements are, and shows how Role Activity Diagrams (RADs) model them. Drawing on Praxis' own experience with RADs we also comment on the capture and subsequent analysis of process models.

WHY PROCESS MODELLING?

Business Process Engineers are interested in the way people work together to achieve business objectives, generally with a view to making them more effective and more efficient. Process models can help them in several ways:

Software Assistance for Business Re-engineering. Edited by Kathy Spurr, Paul Layzell, Leslie Jennison and Neil Richards

(a) As a focus for discussion. A good modelling technique, with sound syntax and semantics, and accompanied by a disciplined process for *doing* the modelling, will help us ask the right questions about the real world and tease out the important points for discussion and agreement.

(b) As a means for communicating a process to others. People not involved in developing the model may review it or use it as a basis for approving a new or changed process. A model of an approved process may serve as a guide to those who have to carry it out.

(c) As a basis for analysis. Analysis of the model can reveal weak points in the process, for example actions that add little value or are potential bottlenecks. Given suitable animation and simulation tools, the model may be used to explore the effects of changes.

(d) For designing a new process.

(e) As a baseline for continuing process improvement. Suggestions for change can be expressed as changes to the model. For those interested in collecting metrics, a model is not only necessary for a clear understanding of what the metrics mean, but the model may itself suggest useful things to measure.

(f) As a program for controlling the real world process. A sufficiently formal model may be used to drive an *enaction* system, such as a Workflow Management System. This executes the process within a computer system and can ensure that the process is carried out faithfully every time it is used, that deadlines are met, and that accurate metrics and audit trails are kept automatically.

WHAT MAKES A GOOD PROCESS MODEL?

Models are a means of showing the essentials of complex problems. They allow us to abstract from the real world, highlighting those objects and relationships which are of interest and ignoring those that are not. What are the relevant abstractions for assisting Business Process Engineers?

Curtis *et al.* (1992) classify them into four *perspectives*:

- *Functional*, representing what *activities* are being performed and what *dataflows* connect them.

- *Behavioural*, representing *when* activities are performed, with sequencing, feedback loops, iteration, decision making, triggering conditions, etc.

- *Organisational*, representing *where* and by *whom* activities are performed, plus physical communication mechanisms and storage media.

- *Informational*, representing the data *entities* involved in a process, including their structure and interrelationships.

The key perspectives for the Business Process Engineer are the *behavioural* and *organisational* ones. The rules that govern sequencing and decision-making are at the very heart of the process, and the parts that people play in the process are exactly the components that are likely to be rearranged when it comes to improving the process. Many people are using (and selling) little more than Data Flow Diagramming techniques for "process modelling"; these only address the *functional* perspective. It is possible to use several different modelling techniques to cover all perspectives, but then they need to be integrated in some way. Some form of automated repository can help avoid inconsistencies, but this still leaves the problem of integrating the different perspectives in one's head—essential for a thorough understanding of the process.

Other characteristics of a good modelling technique are, we suggest:

- The models should be diagrammatic rather than textual, since that makes them easier to comprehend and manipulate.

- The objects and relationships represented in the model should be intuitively familiar, so that people can readily understand and talk about them with little training (though we can allow the *drawing* of the diagrams to need a higher level of skill).

- The modelling notation should have formal syntax and semantics so that it can be analysed and, possibly, enacted.

- It should be possible to handle *complexity*.

PROCESS MODELLING WITH STRIM

STRIM has been developed at Praxis as the process modelling component of the Touche Ross approach to Business Process Re-engineering. It addresses the functional, behavioural and organisational perspectives listed above. (The informational perspective is covered separately with traditional entity relationship modelling techniques, and will not be pursued further in this paper.)

The STRIM perspective

STRIM takes the view that there are five key concepts that need to be modelled for a business process:

1. What the organisation is trying to achieve with the process: the business *goals*.
2. What constraints the organisation puts on what people can do and how they should operate: the business *rules*.
3. What individuals do to achieve the goals: *activities*.
4. How activities are divided amongst *roles*.
5. How individuals within groups *interact* collaboratively to get the job done.

Let us look at each of these in turn.

The process goals

For instance, the goal of a process might be to maintain positive cash flow, to manage a research budget, or to get an expense claim paid. It must be possible to see from our process models how a process is achieving the objectives or goals set for it, and, ideally, to be able to identify the point(s) in the process where those goals can be said to have been achieved or maintained.

Goal is in fact a special case of the more fundamental concept of *state*: a goal may be thought of as a state that the process is trying to get to. Ordinary users may not be aware of the concept of state, but in fact they use it all the time; the cry "Where have you got to with my expense claim?" is a question about what state a process is in, and the question "Are we all agreed?" is an attempt to confirm that a key state has been reached.

The business rules

The activities in an organisational process are carried out according to a particular logic when the process "runs", that logic being what the "business rules" are all about. Business rules are the way that activity in the organisation is constrained. These rules can take a number of forms:

- *Policy*. A company might have a policy of buying in the management of its computer facilities.

- *Procedures.* Many organisational activities are regulated and defined in the form of procedures. For example there may be closely defined procedures for planning projects, reporting project status, and purchasing. These procedures are there because the company wishes to control commitment—especially financial commitment—closely. Procedures can also exist to make interfaces efficient: all requests for training follow the same procedure so that people requesting training do not need to invent how to make a request, and the people handling requests know in what form they will arrive.

- *Standards.* Standards are often laid down to define a common appearance or layout for something produced during the process. In Praxis, project plans and reports conform to a standard layout. The reasons for such standardisation are again twofold: efficiency—everyone knows what a report looks like and where to find the information they are interested in; and control—we want to ensure that certain topics always get covered and certain information is always included.

- *Responsibility levels, authorisation and delegation mechanisms.* These prescribe who can do what: who can sign off purchases above what value, who can authorise a change in production schedules, who can cancel a project, who can delegate what to whom.

All these are rules that govern "how things get done around here", and we need to be able to capture them in our process models.

Individuals do things

We must be able to capture the productive actions that people carry out, such as checking an expense claim, or issuing a payment.

Processes are divided over roles

A role is a set of activities that are generally carried out by an individual or group with some organisationally relevant responsibility. Associated with the role are the resources required for performing that role, such as files, desks, tools, and skills.

For example, an important role may be that of *project managing*. This role would be *acted* by one person at a time, and within the role there are many activities that that person would undertake: planning, reporting, monitoring, managing staff, liaising with suppliers, working with the client, and so on. The role of managing project X could be acted by me today, and by another person tomorrow. The role is separate from the people who act it.

One's first inclination when naming roles is to use names like *Project Manager*, though this can make it too seductive to identify roles with job functions, forgetting that job functions are invariably made up of activities that often contribute to a number of different processes. For instance, the job function "Managing Director" could be thought of as a role, but it is clearly a function that has a part to play in many processes in the company's activity: as authoriser of large purchase orders, as setter of the company's strategy, and as an important part of maintaining the company's relationship with its clients.

Equally, it is tempting to identify parts of the organisation as roles: departments, divisions, sections, or whatever. For instance, "Reception" could be thought of as a role, but we can also view Reception as a group of people who contribute to several processes in the company: they may act as Goods Inwards clerks and hence contribute to the purchasing process; as the people who answer telephone calls and greet guests they are part of the marketing process. Similarly, a Finance Department, though forming a readily identifiable group of people, might actually participate in a number of separate though related processes including remunerating staff (by paying people), purchasing (by paying suppliers), and handling the company's cash-flow (by invoicing clients, chasing bad debts, and negotiating with banks).

Whether or not we associate job titles or parts of the organisation with roles will, like so many similar decisions, depend on why we are modelling the process. Roles can be manifested in many ways, including:

- a functional group: Accounts
- a job title: Project Manager
- a functional position or post: Financial Director
- a person: Peter Extonbury
- a class of person: Customer
- an abstraction: Expense claimant

Some process models that we have prepared for clients have had, on a single page, roles from each of the different sorts.

Roles are the most important concepts in STRIM process modelling. They allow us to abstract subsets of activities carried out by a person as a coherent whole. A role runs independently, with its own set of resources (such as specific skills, files, reference material), and coordinates with other roles as necessary, via *interactions*.

Roles interact

People (acting in some role) do not only operate as independent individuals. Processes almost invariably involve the collaboration of a number of individuals or groups, and that collaboration takes place through many sorts of interaction, such as

- I pass you some information
- I delegate a task to you
- We agree on an action
- You pass me the results of your work
- I wait for you to do something

Roles may wait, collect, check, monitor, chase, ... a multiplicity of apparently "non-productive" activities which, it is to be hoped, further the process they are part of. Management activity is particularly composed of such activities carried out to organise or facilitate a process.

In the process of Claiming Expenses, the role *Expense claimant* will need to interact with the role *Accounts* to get them to pay the claim and the *Accounts* role will want to obtain approval from the *Financial Director* role to pay expenses over a certain amount. In the process of Developing a Portfolio of Products, the role *Board of Directors* will want to pass a statement of direction to the *Product Strategy Board* along with a budget level and targets. In return, the *Product Strategy Board* will present the *Board of Directors* with information on the chosen portfolio, and report progress against budget and targets.

An interaction is neutral and has no implied direction—it is just some coordination between roles. It often involves the transfer of something, some entity—what we call a *gram*—from the sphere of concern of one role to that of the other. For example, the *Expense claiming* role will interact with the *Accounts* role so that the expense claimant can pass over their expenses claim for processing. In some cases there will be an exchange of grams: I give you money in return for goods. But an interaction need not involve the transfer of a gram at all: for instance, you and I might interact simply to agree on something—"nothing changes hands".

An interaction can be two-party, involving two roles, or multi-party, involving a number of roles. However many parties are involved, interactions are always *synchronous*; that is, all the participating roles must be ready for the interaction to take place before it can start, it starts at the same moment for each party, and it completes at the same moment for each party. In some cases an interaction might physically take a few seconds

(I give you an expenses claim), in others months (a vendor and purchaser agree on the contractual terms of a sale).

What about data?

At this point, you might well ask "why is *data* or *information* not in this list of concepts?". It is our experience that the data most necessary to a process (and therefore worthy of modelling) is readily revealed by examining the process alone. This will generally be data that is the subject matter of someone's activity, such as a design or a plan, or the subject matter of an interaction between two people. Much data that is seen around organisations either records the state of a process (because people have poor memories) or is just a way of implementing interactions. For example, an order-processing system would hold a lot of information about the state of each order; but when we model the order-processing process we do not need to model the process *and* the data that would be necessary to record its state; the latter is only necessary for an implementation. Similarly, data such as an invoice is only a physical means of implementing an interaction: namely a vendor requesting payment from a purchaser. It might be quite irrelevant to the process whether a paper invoice or EDI or a phone call is used in effecting the interaction. The interaction is important; the way data is used might be incidental.

Representing the process

STRIM includes two languages for modelling processes—a textual language, *SPML*, and a diagrammatic language in the form of a *Role Activity Diagram* (RAD).

SPML is derived from RML (Greenspan, 1984). We will not discuss it further in this paper; the interested reader may refer to Ould and Roberts (1988) for a demonstration of the use of a RAD and RML to model a simple process.

RADs are based on Petri net theory and were first described by Holt *et al.* (1983) in the context of modelling software engineering processes; Praxis has adapted them slightly.

The notation for RADs is summarised in Figure 1. The concepts of *role, activity, goal* (as a state to be reached) and *interaction* are represented directly. The business *rules* show up as the pattern of sequencing, decision-making and concurrent activity that binds them all together.

Figure 2 is a RAD for a typical expense claiming process. Time proceeds

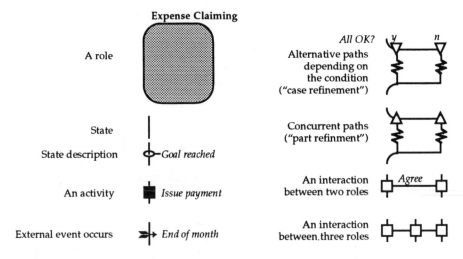

Figure 1   The RAD notation

downwards in a RAD. To read it, start at the top of each role and work down the vertical line. Activities (black boxes) are carried out as you come to them. Each role proceeds in its own time, concurrently with the others, until it reaches an interaction. Interactions can only take place when all roles involved get to that point; they all continue together after the interaction.

In Figure 2, when the event *End of month* occurs, the **Expense claimant** is triggered to *Create expenses claim.* He then interacts with one or more **Project Managers** to get their approvals, and sends the completed claim to **Accounts**. At this point, **Accounts** *Check the claim,* with the outcome that it is either:

- rejected as invalid in some way, or
- acceptable and for no more than $1000, or
- acceptable and for more than $1000.

Following the *no* path (for rejection) we see that this results in an interaction with **Expense claimant** to inform him of the rejection. He then modifies the claim and returns to the same state he was in before obtaining **Project Manager** approvals, whence he can try again.

Note that the RAD has abstracted away from any *physical* mechanisms. The RAD is valid whether the Expense Claim is sent around on paper or by email.

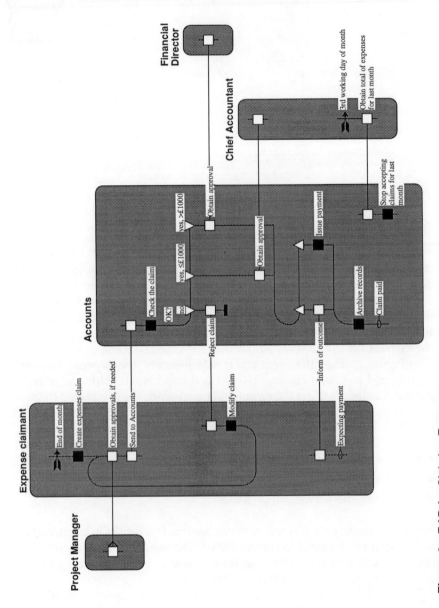

Figure 2 RAD for Claiming Expenses

HOW TO CAPTURE A PROCESS

So far we have discussed the concepts and (briefly) the notation of process modelling. But we also need a way of going about *doing* the modelling (a process for process modelling, if you like). This paper is not the place to go into this in great detail, but there are some important general points to be made, as answers to the following questions:

1. How do I gather information to build my model?
2. How do I handle complexity?
3. How will I know when my model is complete?

How do I gather information to build my model?

Let us assume that we wish to model an existing process. The STRIM analyst gathers facts principally by interviewing those who carry out the process, ideally as a group. The aim of the questioning is to flush out the roles, activities, entities, and role interactions that form the organisation's process. At each stage, the business rules and goals that govern the process are also recorded. A series of questions can be asked under a number of general headings:

- What is the overall organisational structure and its business goals?
- What do people *do* in their separate roles?
- How do the roles interact?
- What entities are essential to the process? Data that records state is not important for this modelling.

As well as conducting interviews and group sessions to elicit this information, the analyst can use all the traditional techniques for finding out what is going on in an organisation. These include:

- *Examining existing documents.* For example, distribution lists represent potential interactions, whether or not they serve a useful purpose.
- *Examining the contents of people's in- and out-trays.* Again we are looking for interactions.
- *Examining existing procedures manuals, work instructions, Quality Manuals, etc.* These can be an important source for the analyst, but we need to be

careful that the processes described therein are the ones that are actually carried out. Are we modelling how it is *supposed* to be done, or how it is *actually* done?

We have done process modelling on a whiteboard with the group of people who actually carry out the process: the expert modeller facilitating the modelling by the untrained user. We have also done it by first carrying out interviews with individuals who have their own part to play in the process, and then going away to draw the models separately. Where possible we like to start by getting an overall picture, no matter how coarse or inaccurate, and this can be done either by getting the group together for say half a day (this is often logistically difficult), or by interviewing someone who has a good grasp of the whole process even though they might only operate a part of it. This overall model usually has "large" roles each containing several disconnected threads of activity that, at a more detailed level, will turn out to be roles in their own right.

It is important to get representative views of *all* participants in the process. It is dangerous, for example, to rely solely on a supervisor's view of the process carried out by their juniors.

RAD notation is intuitively straightforward and we find that people readily model in it, provided that the analyst actually does the drafting for them on a whiteboard. The notation is sufficiently transparent for people to work with their *process* during a modelling session, rather than working on (struggling with) the notation.

People find it much easier to describe what they do in terms of RAD interactions rather than (for example) the artificial "dataflows" that DFD modelling demands: the user is more likely to say "I ask Accounts for the total expenses figure for the month" rather than "I send Accounts a total-of-expenses request".

How do I handle complexity?

The traditional systems analyst's models like DFDs, ELHs and Jackson structure charts are the products of software engineering minds, and software engineers (and the vendors of software engineering tools) are very fond of hierarchically structured things—they are amenable to elegant, simple and well understood handling. As a result the models themselves take the form of hierarchies ("levelling" in DFDs), which is a good way of dealing with complexity.

Unfortunately, organisational processes do not necessarily fit into a neat structured decomposition. In fact, rather than being hierarchical, processes tend to be multi-dimensional networks. (Looking at business processes in software engineering terms, we observe that this is because they include notions of concurrency and interrupts—always difficult to model in the standard notations.)

What, then, happens if we "open" a black box on a RAD? Rather than seeing a "decomposition" of that activity, we prefer to say that we are looking through a window and seeing part of the process from another perspective. What we see and what we model depends again on why we are modelling. For instance, take the activity *Issue payment* in Figure 2. Suppose we open this black box. When we look through it we may find a whole world of process there involving, in particular, new roles such as *Bank*, and *Post Room*. These do not appear on the first RAD, nor are they "part of" any of the roles therein. In taking *Issue payment* as a process in its own right, we are starting to look at new parts of the world, parts that we were not interested in when drawing up the original RAD.

The same applies to interactions. As an example, take a simplification of this interaction: "Two parties, *A* and *B*, meet to discuss, negotiate and agree the price of a piece of work, drawing up the agreement as a legal document and obtaining financial securities from a bank". On a RAD we might choose to represent this as an atomic interaction between roles *A* and *B* because we are not interested in that model in any further "detail"—we simply want to say that *A* and *B* have that interaction with that result, and we don't mind how they do it.

Suppose we now choose to "open up" this interaction. Rather than showing just more detail of what happens between *A* and *B*, we will find other roles involved, roles which perhaps did not appear on the first RAD: *Bank Manager, Giving legal advice, Auditor* for example. We have not decomposed the atomic interaction in the DFD sense: we have opened it up and looked at the process from a new angle, an angle which introduces new roles and perhaps new entities, all of which were of no interest to the first RAD.

How will I know when my model is complete?

Suppose we want to measure the length of the coastline of an island. If there is a road around the island we could drive round it and use the vehicle's odometer. We could get a "more accurate" (and larger, and more time-consuming) answer by walking around the coastline with a pedometer, dipping into each inlet and around each promontory along the coastal path.

This is a good metaphor for process modelling. There is always more detail if you want to look for it. Whether the detail is useful and justifies the expense of collection, only the process modeller can determine—there is no simple rule that can tell you "you have finished!". Completeness is in the eye of the modeller.

In fact things are more complicated than this. *There is no single viewpoint of a process.* It will vary as our motives vary. If we are interested in why a process seems to have a bottleneck around certain activities we will want to model the process from the point of view of how work is allocated to individuals. If we are interested in how the functional subdivisions of the organisation impede or facilitate the flow of a transaction through a process that crosses functional boundaries we will want to view the process in terms of those boundaries. There are as many models of a single process as there are viewpoints that we might want to take.

In our work for a pharmaceutical company, we initially prepared two models of the same process, seeing it from two viewpoints: one from that of the scientists doing the science necessary to take a new compound to market, another from that of the management pushing the development of the compound through the various stages of process scale-up and trials whilst weeding out those compounds that do not offer future success. In *Soft Systems* terms (Checkland and Scholes, 1992) these views are *holons* which we "put against the world" in order to learn about it. Each corresponds to a different idea of the "purposeful activity" of the process.

We conclude that it is essential that the modeller have in mind some clear purpose for drawing the model, and some idea of the boundaries of the model.

HOW TO ANALYSE A PROCESS

It is our experience that much is learnt about a process, to the benefit of the business, simply by going through the exercise of creating a RAD. Concentrated thinking about the process in a disciplined way together with the bringing together of different perceptions often brings out obvious improvements.

Common sense plays a large part in analysing a process for improvement, but we also need techniques for analysing the model in a systematic way. These fall into the two broad categories of *qualitative* and *quantitative* analysis.

Qualitative analysis

We should ask these questions about the objects and relationships represented on the RAD:

- *Goals*: Are they all identified? Are they met?

- *Roles*: Are there roles that have few activities of their own, seeming to be only third-parties in other roles' interactions? They may be redundant, adding no value, and slowing the process.

- *Interactions*: Is the interaction necessary? Is is a bottleneck? We can borrow ideas from speech act theory (Auramaki *et al.*, 1992) and check the *commitments* that are being made when an interaction occurs. We will be looking, for example, for delegation without feedback, implicit promises that are not kept, information that is transferred but not used.

Quantitative analysis

Some simple metrics of the efficiency of the process may be derived by counting the numbers of actions and interactions. A process (or role) with fewer interactions or a lower ratio of interactions to actions is likely to be better: each interaction is a potential bottleneck while waiting for synchronisation.

By adding numerical properties such as duration and effort to actions and interactions, we can calculate total process time. Techniques based on traditional network planning or Monte Carlo simulation can be applied.

TOOL SUPPORT

Tool support for drawing RADs is available. At Praxis we are using *RADitor*, from Co-Ordination Systems Ltd. Support for quantitative analysis is being developed.

EXAMPLES OF USE

At Praxis we have been using the STRIM techniques described here on various client assignments:

- Making a detailed model of the process of chemical development in a pharmaceutical company as a basis for examining the possibility of automating certain aspects and for re-engineering parts of the process to be more stringently controlled.

- Assisting managers in a major computer manufacturer to model the process it used for planning its product portfolio and for monitoring the progress of development of each individual product. The simple objective was to establish just what the process actually was and to gain common understanding and agreement as to how it should run. A particular concern was to capture the business rules that governed who could do what.

- For another organisation, as part of the development of a Quality Management System, we modelled all Information Systems processes, including service development, service maintenance, service operation, and those at the top management level. The aim was to document the processes using RADs as a basis for assigning quality controls and authorisation levels, for disseminating via a Quality Manual, and subsequent improvement.

- We modelled a decision-making process related to the granting of credit by a client, with the aim of identifying those parts in the process where Knowledge Based Systems techniques could be applied.

Additionally, within Praxis, we have used RADs to illustrate our own key business processes—including project planning and reporting, purchasing, change control, and bid management—in our Quality Manual.

CONCLUSION

In this paper we have attempted to give an introduction to an effective approach to process modelling, using Role Activity Diagrams. Be warned, however, that, in the words of Holt *et al.* (1983): "The content and implications of roles and interactions are not easy to grasp quickly. Only through training and practical work is it possible fully to understand their consequences". Our own experience bears this out.

REFERENCES

Auramaki E, Hirschheim R and Lyytinnen K. 1992. Modelling Offices Through Discourse Analysis: The SAMPO Approach. *The Computer Journal*, Vol 35 No 4, August 1992.
Checkland P and Scholes J. 1992. *Soft Systems Methodology in Action*. Wiley, Chichester.

Curtis W, Kellner M I and Over J. 1992. Process Modeling. *Communications of the ACM* September 1992, Vol 35 No 9.

Greenspan S. 1984. *Requirements Modeling: A Knowledge Representation Approach to Software Requirements Definition*. Technical Report CSRG-155, Computer Systems Research Group, University of Toronto.

Holt A W, Ramsey H R and Grimes J D. 1983. Coordination System Technology as the Basis for a Programming Environment. *ITT Technical Journal (Electrical Communication)*, Vol 557 No 4.

Ould M A and Roberts C. 1988. Defining formal models of the software development process. In: Brereton P (Ed) *Software Engineering Environments 1987*, Ellis Horwood, Chichester.

7

Strategic Business Process Engineering: A Systems Thinking Approach Using ithink

Richard Stevenson

ABSTRACT

Business process engineering, re-engineering, re-design, etc., are all terms which have emerged in the 1990s to describe a new management approach whose aim is to achieve *substantial* improvements in customer service and efficiency. The *focus* is to rethink and to streamline the processes by which organisations create and deliver *value*. The *object* is to design organisations which consistently deliver needed products and services to customers, at required quality, on time, and at least cost. Processes are the operational activities which must meet these requirements and process *structure* is the key to organisational *performance*.

This paper suggests that, too often, process improvement initiatives still start at sub-levels within organisations. Yet localised or uncoordinated process initiatives can prove positively *damaging* to overall performance.

Software Assistance for Business Re-engineering. Edited by Kathy Spurr, Paul Layzell, Leslie Jennison and Neil Richards
© 1993 John Wiley & Sons Ltd

The challenge to managers and practitioners is to develop new tools and techniques which facilitate a *high level*, coordinated approach and active participation in process engineering by top people in the organisation.

The conceptual framework and techniques of "systems thinking" provide a relevant high level methodology for process engineering by managers. In particular, the methodology provides techniques and tools for process *simulation*—the only risk-free way to explore relationships between process structure and organisational performance.

Criteria to help managers select simulation tools which support process engineering are proposed. One suitable tool—ithink?—is described and its use in management-led approaches to process modelling and organisational design is outlined.

The methodology is illustrated by an example in UK health care and social services, using ithink to build simple graphical maps and simulation models which relate process structure to problematic process behaviour. The example also illustrates the absolute necessity of adopting a high-level approach in process engineering.

INTRODUCTION: PROCESS ENGINEERING REQUIRES NEW MANAGEMENT THINKING

Process Engineering—A High-Level Activity

The major quality breakthrough of the 1980s was not just-in-time, nor total quality management, nor any other exotic quality technique. It was the realisation by management that business and manufacturing processes are the key to customer service and to organisational performance. This *structural* perspective offers a no-nonsense blueprint for performance improvement which transcends low-level, often bureaucratic, quality management techniques. Business process engineering (or re-engineering, etc.) is a high-level approach, concerned with *designing* organisations which work.

Processes are *operational* activities which deliver value to customers. The object [1] of process engineering is to:

a) Make processes *effective*—produce desired results
b) Make processes *efficient*—minimise resources
c) Make processes *adaptable*—to changing customer and business needs.

The effectiveness of core processes, and *interactions* between them, determine whether and how organisations can achieve their objectives.

It follows that process design is of *strategic* importance and requires high-level management direction and participation.

Process Engineering: Low-Level Deficiencies

The whole point of process engineering is to improve organisational performance overall. The trouble is that many organisations were designed with *functional* building blocks (in truth, most organisations were not actually designed at all) and processes run *through* functions. And because functional management predominates, many process improvement initiatives still start at sub-levels within organisations, tackle processes in a staged or piecemeal fashion, or for other reasons fail to establish proper linkages between core business processes. As we shall see, low-level process interventions can cause significant problems, and may even make overall performance *worse*.

Process Engineering: New Thinking Challenges

Performance improvement via process engineering requires that two major thinking challenges be met by organisations:

a) *Localised Thinking.* Most managers work day-to-day within functional boundaries. But organisational performance results from interrelationships which play out across functional boundaries as well as the boundary between the organisation and its environment. Process improvement initiatives applied within narrowly defined boundaries usually result only in moving problems on—they quickly re-emerge elsewhere, often in a different form. Thus local process improvement initiatives may actually make overall performance *worse*.

b) *Short Term Thinking.* Most organisations and managers operate with short time horizons. Pressures for immediate performance improvements lie uncomfortably with the fact that the results of radical process changes may take many months or even years to eventuate. Indeed, it is an uncomfortable fact that things often need to get worse before they can get better!

Organisations must recognise that a commitment to process engineering will require adjustments to both their spacial and temporal perspectives.

In particular, such adjustments will require all managers, across the functional disciplines, to think *systemically* and *dynamically*.

To make the transition, managers will need *both* a sound and relevant conceptual framework by which they can share their knowledge and experience with colleagues, *and* new tools to help them to learn together how real and lasting improvements may be achieved.

SYSTEMS THINKING—A RELEVANT FRAMEWORK FOR PROCESS ENGINEERING

System Dynamics and Systems Thinking

Interest in *processes* as building blocks of organisational structure is a relatively recent shift in mainstream management thinking. But the process perspective of management systems has been with us for over thirty years within the framework of *system dynamics*, originally developed by Jay Forrester [2] at the Massachusetts Institute of Technology. System dynamics is concerned with creating *simulation* models of real world systems of all kinds in order to study their dynamic behaviour. The purpose is to develop understanding of relationships between the underlying *structure* of a system, its *policies* (decision rules) and its *behaviour* (performance over time).

A wider term, *systems thinking*, has more recently been used by Senge [3] and others to describe a conceptual framework and a body of management knowledge deriving substantive content from the disciplines of system dynamics. Systems thinking may be described as "a rigorous method for exploring and understanding complex systems in terms of *processes, information feedback, delays, organisational boundaries and policies.*" This theme will be developed later in this paper.

Systems Thinking is Relevant to Organisations

Organisations may legitimately be considered as complex systems, whose behaviours are governed by networks of interrelated actions which often take years to fully play out. And process changes in organisations— particularly the radical changes implied by process engineering—should be carried out from a basis of *understanding* of organisational behaviour derived from systemic principles.

Systems thinking is a sound and relevant methodology to facilitate understanding by managers of the way their organisations really work.

The methodology supports the object of *designing* business processes to deliver strategies which achieve organisational goals.

THE ROLE OF SIMULATION IN PROCESS ENGINEERING AND ORGANISATIONAL DESIGN

Jay Forrester recently proposed[4] that the future role of top management will be that of corporate *designers* rather than corporate *operators*—their objective will be to create organisations in which ordinarily competent people can succeed. Often, we see people in organisations blamed for failures when the fault really lies in the situations in which they have been placed. Much of the time, it is the design of the organisation which is defective—usually in respect of misalignment of its core processes.

A parallel may be drawn with science and engineering. In designing a new chemical plant or a passenger jetliner, for example, engineers recognise the complexity of the task; design cannot be left to experience or rules of thumb. Before even a prototype is built, computer models are used to *simulate* system behaviour over a wide range of conditions. Managers and engineers work together to analyse the outcomes of simulations and to discuss design implications. Modifications are proposed, more simulations are conducted, designs are progressively improved. The design team *learns* about relationships between system structure and system behaviour. When the first prototype is built, there is usually a high probability that it will "fly".

By total contrast, managerial and social systems usually emerge through informal methods. Although political, economic and management systems are far more complex than engineering systems, the design methodology is usually based on experience, intuition and informal debate. And there is plenty of evidence that organisational "designers" often get it wrong!

There is no reason why organisations cannot be designed in broadly the same way as other complex systems. This is not to deny the need for human judgment—but judgment can be very significantly enhanced by the use of simulation, which is the *only* way to learn how a redesigned process will behave without "betting the company" by implementing changes in the real system.

The challenge is to design operational processes which align with the organisation's vision and its strategies—hence to design processes which really *can* deliver on strategies, i.e. to design organisations that will "fly". Systems thinking provides a sound conceptual framework and a simulation methodology to support this high-level objective.

SELECTION OF SIMULATION TOOLS TO SUPPORT PROCESS ENGINEERING

Simulation Tools and Languages

Various computer-based tools exist which facilitate process simulation. However, most simulation tools are discrete-event languages which are adequate for modelling at low levels of detail but unsuitable for providing high-level perspectives of organisations. Worse, most of these tools require expert analysts to use them—they exclude effective participation by managers in model construction, which is where the real *learning* occurs.

Process Modelling Tools—Selection Criteria

It may be useful to propose some criteria which should be considered in selecting process modelling tools for use not (only) by analysts but by managers who have to understand how changes to processes will actually improve organisational performance.

a) *Sound Conceptual Framework.* To be credible to managers, tools need a convincing conceptual framework which should be sufficiently *simple* to describe system and process structures in terms which can be readily grasped, sufficiently *rigorous* to provide a clear link between structure and dynamic behaviour, and sufficiently *generic* to describe a wide range of systems and processes.

b) *High Level Perspective.* Modelling tools should be capable of describing corporate strategies *and* the operational processes which underlie them. This implies a "high level" perspective—which can first capture a *minimum* level of detail consistent with reality but has the capability to disaggregate progressively to lower levels of detail *as necessary.*

   Many quality projects start with low-level mapping activities—this is often the case in TQM projects, for example. Most "bottom-up" mapping—which captures a lot of detail without clear objectives—is a waste of effort and management time.

c) *Dynamic Capabilities.* It is common that process behaviour in the short term may be different from longer term behaviour—process changes which appear to provide short term benefits may even be damaging if viewed with a different time horizon.

   Most people find it difficult to think through the dynamics of process *behaviour*—yet many people are good at describing process *structure* in maps and diagrams. It should therefore be possible to describe system structures in maps, then to translate the same maps directly into simulation models which help managers to understand consequential dynamic behaviour.

d) *"Language" Discipline.* Seeing *relationships* within and between processes is vital to understanding structure and behaviour. This need implies a mapping language having a symbol set which is simple, comprehensive and wholly consistent in its ability to describe very different processes. For example, the same symbol set should be equally capable of mapping problems in production logistics, administrative work processes, manpower planning, sales and marketing strategies, etc.

e) *Closed-Loop Perspective of Structure.* Most mapping tools and simulation languages treat structural relationships within processes as if they were linear or "open loop" (see Figure 1). In fact, close examination of any real world process will reveal that relationships are in fact circular (see Figure 2).

Feedback loops are fundamental components of processes—indeed any process which did *not* contain feedback would quickly rage out of control. It is vital to capture feedback relationships in order to understand how processes will behave.

Figure 1   Open Loop View of the World

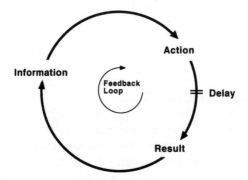

Figure 2   Closed Loop View of the World

f) *Management-friendly Graphical Interface.* High-level process engineering methods and tools must be used in the boardroom rather than the back room!

This implies that models must be driven from a graphical interface—very few managers have the time or inclination to learn complex programming languages. Ideally, it should be possible to construct and run models directly from graphical "maps" of process structures, drawn on a computer screen.

g) *Learning and Communication.* At the end of the day, process changes have to be implemented—often by different managers from those who do the planning.

Modelling tools should therefore facilitate clear communication of process-improvement initiatives to those not directly concerned in the planning activity. Process maps and simulation models are the best way to disseminate insights—far more effective than written reports, for example.

Few process modelling tools in present use match up to these demanding requirements. The remainder of this paper discusses one tool—ithink—which scores highly under every one of the issues discussed above.

ithink—A PROCESS MODELLING TOOL FOR MANAGERS

Introduction

This section provides a short overview of the concepts and practical methodologies which underpin ithink, a modelling tool derived from system dynamics. ithink was developed specifically to provide a way to link system structure to dynamic behaviour.

ithink is designed primarily for use by managers. A powerful simulation tool, it has been designed to be easy to understand and to use. ithink uses a generic mapping language and is accessed via a graphical interface which facilitates management-led applications.

Experience of using ithink in many situations has shown that managers quickly learn the basics of the tool and that it is very effective at accelerating learning in management teams. Indeed, many managers find that working in multi-functional teams with a tool which allows them to express and explore ideas in a common language, is at once challenging, enjoyable and intensely rewarding.

Conceptual Framework and Language

Systems thinking is a framework for exploring complex systems in terms of five building blocks—*processes, information feedback, delays, organisational boundaries and policies.* Since ithink is designed to support systems thinking, it will be useful to describe the structure and application of ithink in terms of these building blocks.

Building Blocks—(1) Process Structure. The following definition of process structure is taken from the ithink Continuous Process Improvement Module[5]:

"Viewed from the perspective of systems thinking. . ., a process exists when material and/or information is *flowing* through a sequence of *activities,* with each activity resulting in some transformation or storage of the resources that are flowing. Because not all activities in the sequence proceed at the same pace, because from time to time activities cease (voluntarily or involuntarily), and because activities must be fuelled by stored resources, processes also necessarily include *accumulations.*"

Within this framework, two—and *only* two—kinds of process variables exist:

a) *Stocks.* Stocks are accumulations of process resources. At any point in time, it is possible to identify and measure the stocks within a process.

b) *Flows.* Flows are activity variables which directly increase or deplete stocks; their dimensions are usually in units per period of time.

The existence of only two kinds of variables—stocks and flows—is true of *all* processes. This idea should not be new to managers—accounting reports follow the same principle! Balance sheet variables are stocks; profit and loss variables are flows, which cause the balance sheet variables to change.

Figure 3 illustrates how ithink uses these concepts to create a simple, graphical, process mapping "language".

ithink depicts process *stocks* as rectangles. The pipe arrows represent the *flows.* The cloud symbol represents external *boundaries* of the model.

It may be noted that, since stocks and flows are totally generic concepts, the language provides the basis for describing any type of process.

Building Blocks—(2) Information Feedback. Process stocks and flows always exist within information *feedback* loops. Feedback fundamentally determines the behaviour of all real world systems. A decision in a

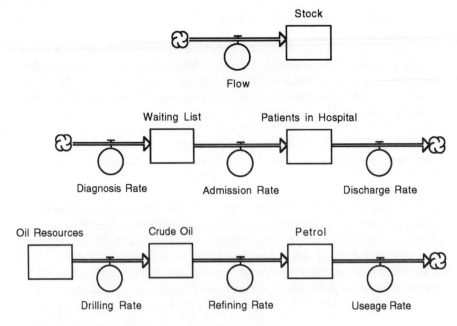

Figure 3 īthink Language of Stocks and Flows

system causes some variable—e.g., employment, cash, product quality—
to change, which affects the next round of decision-making. There is no
beginning and no end—each decision creates an outcome which influences
future decisions.

Feedback loops are of only two kinds:

a) *Positive* (reinforcing) feedback loops, which generate change or growth
    in systems. Examples of outcomes produced by positive feedback
    include compound interest, population growth, drug addiction, etc.

b) *Negative* (balancing) feedback loops, which act to negate change, i.e. to
    close a gap between a variable and a target (explicit or implicit) for the
    variable. Examples of negative feedback include temperature control
    by thermostat, regulation of prices in monopoly industries, cost control
    by budgeting, etc.

A detailed description of feedback is beyond the scope of this paper.
Suffice to say that all real world systems contain *multiple* feedback loops,
and that the interaction of positive and negative loops over time produces
the behaviour exhibited by every system.

The ïthink language needs only two more objects to represent the information and feedback structure of systems. These are the "converter" (used as an input or score keeping variable), and the "connector" (which carries information around the system). Figure 4 illustrates information and feedback loops in ïthink.

Note that the single line arrow (the connector) is fundamentally different from the pipe arrow (the flow). Whereas flows carry "stuff" into and out of stocks, connectors *only* carry information. Think of a connector as carrying electricity rather than water, for example.

Building Blocks—(3) Delays. Delays are important in system behaviour. Frequently there is a delay between the start and finish of a resource conversion activity. ïthink has several methods of representing delays, the simplest of which is the "conveyor" (a special case of the stock).

The conveyor metaphor is that "stuff" rides along the stock for a period of time, then gets off. In Figure 5, the conveyor is used to represent a training delay between recruiting new staff and their becoming qualified for the job.

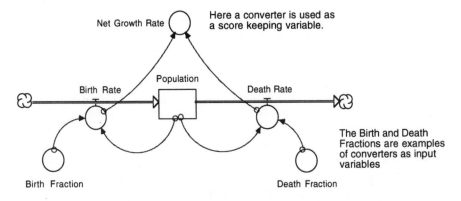

Figure 4   Representing Information and Feedback Structure in ïthink

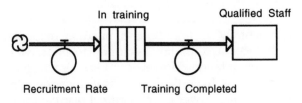

Figure 5   Representing Delays with Conveyors

Note that the conveyor is a high level aggregation device—a convenient way of saying that we are not presently concerned with the *detail* of the training process, only that it exists and results in a delay within a larger process. If at a later stage the training delay is considered to be important, it is possible to "drill down" into the conveyor to build a more detailed map of the training process, i.e. to *disaggregate* the model.

Building Blocks—(4) Boundaries. Organisational boundaries are crucial to process behaviour. Wherever processes move across functional boundaries, different management perspectives, priorities and policies come into play which impact the behaviour of the entire system. It is essential that system and process maps make boundaries *explicit*.

The *external* boundaries of an ithink? model are explicitly defined by "clouds" which appear at the head and/or tail of flows (see Figures 3, 4, and 5). The clouds represent infinite sources or sinks of "stuff"—whatever the cloud represents is assumed to be beyond the current boundary of the model. *Converters* also indicate model boundaries; they represent exogenous assumptions which may need to be challenged.

ithink includes a sector tool to define *internal* boundaries (see Figure 7). It is possible to simulate models sector by sector to assess the nature and extent of cross-boundary interactions.

Building Blocks—(5) Policies. The term *policy* is used here to mean a set of rules which managers use as a basis for decision-making. Policies work through the interaction of feedback loops which create change and/or stabilise performance in the relevant system. ithink's unique ability to explore links between process/feedback structure and dynamic behaviour makes it an ideal tool for policy analysis and design.

Policies must be reflected in the information structure of systems— clearly information structure should support policy design. ithink is particularly powerful in *designing* effective management information structures (MIS) to support policies.

Continuous versus Discrete Event Simulation

ithink is fundamentally a continuous simulation modelling tool, i.e. the software produces a continuous solution to underlying equations which define the simulation. However, ithink also includes discrete-event simulation options. In particular, ithink includes queuing and batch processing facilities which cover the majority of discrete-event modelling requirements.

The issue of whether continuous or discrete-event simulation is most appropriate is purely one of *perspective*. If we are concerned with a high-level, aggregated view of a business or process, continuous simulation is most appropriate. As we disaggregate, individual units (people, batches of material, etc.) become more important. ithink enables modellers to move easily from continuous to discrete simulation, as appropriate.

Process Modelling and Organisational Design with ithink: Project Stages

An overview of a typical ithink based process modelling project will reveal six interrelated stages.

Stage 1—Focus. The first priority in every process-improvement project should be to define a clear operational purpose and expectations for the project. It is rarely useful to "map the process"—this will usually result in large, complex maps which yield few insights yet consume much management time.

The sensible approach is to focus on specific *performance measures* of real concern—then to identify the key elements which drive the performance. This way, it is possible to define clear managerial objectives and to discriminate between essential structure and unnecessary detail.

Stage 2—Mapping. The second stage of an ithink based project is to produce maps (diagrams) which describe the process and information *structure* of the system. ithink maps are constructed directly on the computer screen, using a mouse to "drag" objects into place. Maps are ideally kept simple—the object is to capture the *minimum* amount of process structure needed to shed light on how to improve process behaviour! Good maps are usually small maps—they show the *essence* of process structure rather than every last detail.

Mapping should be driven by process managers—usually only they have sufficient insight to distinguish between essence and unnecessary detail. It may be useful to have an experienced analyst to "facilitate" the mapping process.

Stage 3—Model Construction. In this stage, maps are transformed into quantified models which can be simulated. This is done simply by using the mouse to open each object in the map to enter numerical data or relationships. ithink automatically creates the equation structure which defines the model. At this stage it may be most practical for an analyst to take the model "off-stage" to create the data and relationship structure of the model, although it is by no means beyond the capability of a reasonably numerate manager.

Stage 4—Simulation. Next, models are used to simulate system behaviour. The first priority is to validate the model by re-creating the current, or expected, behaviour of the real-world process. Then the effects of making parameter or structural changes may be explored in careful experimentation.

The results of simulations are displayed in graphs or tables created on the computer screen. It is possible to change a system variable, or modify the structure of the model, then to see the implications of the changes *immediately.*

Simulation provides the opportunity for managers to drive the experimentation process. The ithink model takes on the characteristics of a "learning object"—a focus for intensive discussion and debate.

Stage 5—Iterate! Process modelling with ithink is an intensive learning experience. Learning derives from the interplay created between the structure of process models and the dynamic behaviour which the models produce. Structure creates behaviour, consideration of which leads to changes in structure, which ... until the process improvement team has learned sufficient to progress to the next stage.

Stage 6—Implement! Implementation usually implies a need to convince a wider audience. ithink maps and models capture, in graphic form, the learning which the process-improvement team has experienced and are excellent vehicles for knowledge dissemination.

In practice, an ithink based process modelling project may often be a precursor to more detailed, low level considerations of process design.

CASE EXAMPLE: PROCESS DESIGN IN UK HEALTH CARE AND SOCIAL SERVICES

Introduction

This simple example[6] describes the application of ithink to describe an organisation design problem caused by moving a key process decision variable across a boundary. The purpose of the example is to demonstrate the practical application of ithink? to a real-world (albeit highly simplified) problem, rather than to provide a "solution".

Nevertheless, the *high-level* view provides insights to the problem behaviour which other, more detailed process mapping approaches might not reveal.

Process Description

The processes which move patients across organisational boundaries between the community, the National Health Service (NHS) and Social Services, are crucial to considerations of patient welfare and efficient public spending.

Community care is concerned mainly with elderly, infirm or mentally ill patients, who are often assessed initially for hospital treatment in the NHS before being discharged from hospital into care. All community care is funded by the Department of Social Security. Domiciliary care is delivered by Personal Social Services (PSS) Directorates, and residential care is delivered by the PSS and by the private sector.

Figure 6 shows the simple flow of patients from the community into the NHS (hospitals) and thence to community care (this diagram does not differentiate between domiciliary and residential care). It can be seen that the process will be in balance if the input rate at which patients are assessed to waiting lists ("assessment rate") is the same as the output rate at which patients leave community care ("leaving rate"). The three stocks in the system ("waiting list", "in hospital", "in community care") may to an extent be able to buffer minor changes in input and output rates—in practice the waiting list is the major source of flexibility.

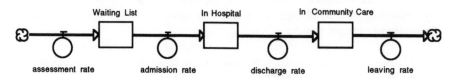

Figure 6   Community Care: Simple Process Structure

Problem Description

Prior to April 1993, the discharge rate from hospitals was solely under the control of the NHS. From April 1993, local PSS groups became responsible for managing all community care under cash-limited budgets. The discharge rate from hospital is now (at least partly) under the control of PSS—if cash resources are limited, the PSS may slow down the discharge of patients from hospitals into community care.

The organisational boundaries within the system are shown in Figure 7, which also shows the process by which costs are accumulated in the community care sector.

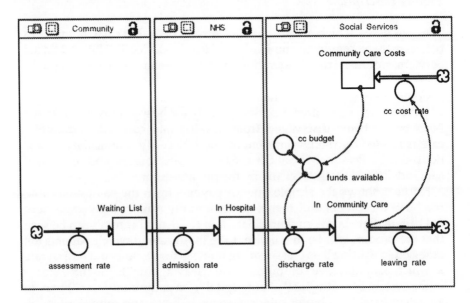

Figure 7   Process Flows and Organisational Boundaries

Now if, due to cash limitations, PSS exercise their budget responsibilities by reducing the discharge rate from hospital, one or more of three consequences must result:

a) Numbers of patients in hospital will rise. In practice, the extent to which this can happen is limited by NHS resources.

b) Waiting lists will increase if NHS consultants reduce the admission rate to ease congestion in hospitals.

c) General practitioners may recognise the problem of hospital congestion and assess fewer people to hospital waiting lists. In this case, some patients who need treatment and care will be denied it.

In practice, all these effects may occur simultaneously. In particular, patients assessed to waiting lists for hospital treatment will remain in the community—but many of them will need domiciliary care while they wait. These people become another drain on the PSS community care budget—the very budget which the original PSS action was intended to control. As the waiting list increases, more money will have to be expended on these patients, leaving less money available for patients already in care. This may, in turn, influence PSS to accept even fewer new patients from the NHS, and so on!

Figure 8 shows the system structure, including policies, which generate this problematic behaviour.

Benefits Derived from Qualitative Mapping using ithink

System maps link process *structure* with system *behaviour*. In particular, maps help to explore how problematic system behaviour arises and may be changed.

Figure 8 shows how the actual outcome of an intended action to impose control within a part of the system, creates an unintended and *opposite* consequence. The *intended* action by PSS is to create a negative (balancing) feedback loop through the discharge rate, to control costs. The *unintended* (but delayed) consequence is to create a positive (reinforcing) loop through the waiting list, counteracting the original action.

This high level ithink map, even in its qualitative form, provides a sound method for charting the potential behaviour of a simple, yet subtly counter-intuitive system. By making explicit the process flows, the system boundaries, and the information feedback loops within the system, the map provides a rich basis for managerial debate.

Further Benefits Derived from Quantitative Modelling (Simulation)

A feature of ithink is that maps can be transformed into simulation models without programming. A working quantified model can be constructed very quickly. The model can be simulated and "results" displayed immediately in graphs or tables on the computer screen. Figure 9 shows an example of graphical output created by ithink from the community care model.

It should be noted that graphs created by simulations are in no sense "forecasts" of real-world system and process behaviour. But they do represent projections of how the system *would* behave, given the assumptions of the model. As such, simulation stimulates debate and accelerates learning about how to improve system behaviour.

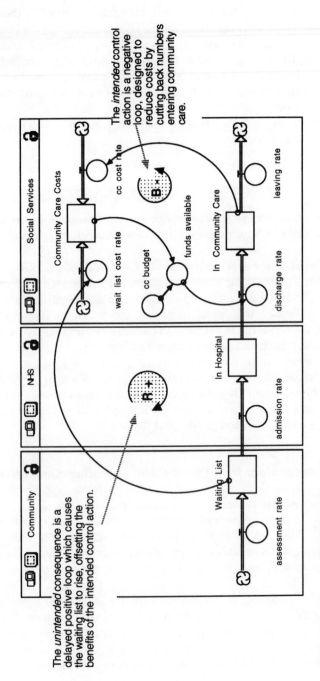

Figure 8 The Unintended Consequence

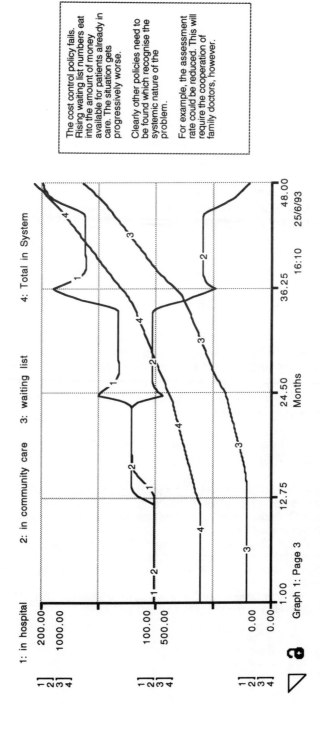

1: in hospital   2: in community care   3: waiting list   4: Total in System

The cost control policy fails. Rising waiting list numbers eat into the amount of money available for patients already in care. The situation gets progressively worse.

Clearly other policies need to be found which recognise the systemic nature of the problem.

For example, the assessment rate could be reduced. This will require the cooperation of family doctors, however.

Graph 1: Page 3

Figure 9 Graphical Output Generated by ithink Simulation

Discussion

The problem is typical of many in process improvement, in that local solutions may not improve performance overall. In this example, a "solution" to the problem is not in the hands of any one of the system "players" (family doctors, NHS, PSS) but will require a *coordinated* approach. Maps and models provide a framework to generate understanding and commitment from all the "players", in cross-functional discussion.

The simple maps and models discussed here are only a *starting point* for investigation of system behaviour which is certainly much more complex than this. Other strategies are available to PSS (reducing costs by cutting the quality of care, for example). These strategies can be superimposed on the model and their effects assessed.

It may be necessary to look at parts of processes in more detail—to investigate what is happening inside hospitals, for example. ithink provides the capability to "disaggregate" the process model without losing the integrity and clarity of the high level map.

Finally, the example demonstrates that *simple*, high level maps and models, derived from a sound conceptual framework, often yield a great deal of insight into process problems and behaviour. The most effective model is usually the simplest that can be constructed, consistent with reality. Process models which dive straight into low levels of detail often miss key performance issues.

REFERENCES

1. *Business Process Improvement*. H. James Harrington. McGraw Hill 1992.
2. *Collected Papers of Jay Forrester*. Wright-Allen Press Inc. 1975.
3. *The Fifth Discipline—The Art and Practice of the Learning Organisation*. Peter M Senge. Doubleday 1990.
4. *"The CEO as Organisational Designer"*. An interview with Professor Jay W Forrester. McKinsey Quarterly. 1992 Number 2.
5. ithink?—*Continuous Process Improvement Module*. High Performance Systems Inc. 1992.
6. *"A Case Study in Community Care using Systems Thinking"*. Eric F Wolstenholme. Paper submitted to the 1993 OR Society Conference.

8

CADDIE: An Advanced Tool for Organisational Design and Process Modelling

Faramarz Farhoodi

ABSTRACT

CADDIE[1] is designed to help the realisation of improved operational effectiveness, improved coordination, and better understanding of costs and benefits of alternative options, in relation to the design/redesign of both human organisations and distributed computer systems. This is achieved by providing support for the definition of users' problems and performance metrics against which alternative solutions can be evaluated.

CADDIE has been developed to address the need for advanced business modelling tools. Building on recent developments in distributed AI, open systems, object-oriented programming and organisational theory,

---

Software Assistance for Business Re-engineering. Edited by Kathy Spurr, Paul Layzell, Leslie Jennison and Neil Richards
© 1994 Logica Cambridge Ltd

[1] CADDIE was a collaborative research project which was supported by the UK Department of Trade and Industry under its Information Engineering Directorate. The project started in March 1990 and was completed in April 1993. The partners in this collaboration were Logica Cambridge Ltd, Dowty Maritime Command & Control Systems and the University of Essex.

CADDIE provides a flexible software tool for enterprise modelling, and in particular, organisational design/redesign. In contrast to purely process-based approaches, CADDIE provides a richer set of business modelling tools which also support behaviour modelling, organisational modelling, effectiveness assessment and environment modelling. CADDIE's facilities can be used to model a business's internal operations and structure, as well as the behaviour of its competitors and its customers.

The second section describes how CADDIE can be used as a modelling tool. The next section discusses an example scenario. The final section contains the concluding remarks.

INTRODUCTION

Overview

New forms of work organisation and corporate management which encourage flexibility and quality of production, whilst retaining the main advantages of standardisation, have been emerging since the 1980s. This is in response to the pressures and opportunities of new technologies and the instability of the international macro-economic environment. CADDIE makes it possible for a business to:

- formulate and compare policies and plans at strategic, tactical and operational levels
- observe the effectiveness and efficiency of its policy, plans and operational procedures against feedback from its internal and external environments
- assess actual performance against its goals and identify corrective actions. These actions range from basic tactical moves (e.g. change price of a product) to complex changes in its organisational structure or procedures (e.g. change from a centralised bureaucracy to a matrix)
- simulate the efficacy of alternative plans and actions and their underlying assumptions, against different scenarios, before these are implemented

CADDIE has been developed to address the need for tools to enable organisational issues to be explored and co-operative working environments to be designed effectively.

Although a number of commercial software packages have been

developed to support the simulation of systems dynamics/process modelling (e.g. ithink, Vensim), there is a distinct lack of practical tools that embody and exploit recent developments in the field of Artificial Intelligence (AI) that are relevant for broader enterprise modelling activities such as organisational modelling; strategic planning, that is, identification of strategic actions to achieve objectives in accordance with an enterprise's mission; and performance assessment.

Typical application areas

CADDIE provides a powerful environment for developing applications in areas where problem-solving activities are inherently distributed, for example:

- Enterprise modelling
- Command and control
- CASE (i.e. the study of alternative distributed software and computer architectures)
- Computer Support for Cooperative Working (CSCW)
- Gaming and simulation

In the following sections, this paper focuses on the use of CADDIE as a modelling tool to support business process and organisational modelling.

Features

Some of the key features of CADDIE for business modelling are as follows:

- CADDIE allows sophisticated modelling of the behaviour of decision makers
- CADDIE is able to model both contiguous and discrete processes
- CADDIE can model stochastic and deterministic processes
- CADDIE facilitates modelling of both social and functional organisation

CADDIE embodies the following technical features:

- Object-oriented architecture. CADDIE's architecture is object-oriented, thus facilitating the development of highly modularised and heterogeneous distributed modelling systems. In CADDIE intelligent objects are called *agents*. An agent is an object that can sense, act and reason. Each agent can have combinations of simple and complex capabilities, which enable it to manage and reason with actions and processes, for example planning, inferencing, communication and negotiation.

- Rich representation of organisational knowledge. This has the potential of enabling CADDIE experimenters to explore complex issues of organisation design. Parameters of an organisation can be varied in order to develop an understanding of its dynamics, and to design efficient and robust control hierarchies.

- Rich representation of knowledge about agents; domain tasks and processes; events; belief; time; uncertainty and various types of constraints and control. A CADDIE agent can embody a rich set of knowledge including self-knowledge, knowledge about intentions and beliefs of other agents, knowledge about how to perform tasks and knowledge about laws of nature and the real-world environment.

- Ease of integration and interfacing with other analysis tools, for example mathematical modelling.

- Advanced simulation support and performance information.

- Support for large scale system development.

USING CADDIE FOR MODELLING

For modelling and simulation applications CADDIE provides a number of facilities for:

- creation of agents with varying capabilities and skills (e.g. a Police Officer with special skills)

- representation of tasks and events which comprise, and are associated with, processes (e.g. purchasing, planning)

- study of different organisation styles and consequences of changing from one style to another (e.g. a centralised hierarchical organisation changing to a matrix type organisation)

- creation and testing of strategic and tactical plans (e.g. alternative ways of improving flexibility within an organisation)

- development and testing of organisational procedures (e.g. how tasks are to be performed)

- studying variations in the distribution of knowledge over agents within an organisation (e.g. assessment of costs vs benefits of distributing certain types of information or centralising them in one place)

- performance monitoring in a scenario (i.e. whether any changes made to the parameters of the simulation improve or worsen its outcome, according to the defined performance metrics)

- perturbation analysis (e.g. study how agents cope with unexpected events).

The next section contains examples of these facilities in the context of a scenario from the domain of emergency services command and control.

Overview of the modelling process in CADDIE

Typically, CADDIE scenarios are based on the following concepts:

- the world to be modelled consists of agents or actors, who, among other things:

  — can be human or machine (multiple humans can take part in CADDIE simulations as a part of the agent community)

  — co-exist with other agents in the 'real-world' environment, about which they can form beliefs

  — have a set of capabilities (which can dynamically change)—i.e. the tasks/actions they can perform (processes comprise collections of tasks)

  — generate objectives/goals for themselves and other agents

  — can plan actions for themselves or other agents to execute

  — execute physical and non-actions. Actions can start processes and produce direct effects, or cause events to happen, in the 'real-world' environment. These events can then affect the executor and/or other agents

  — negotiate with each other

  — join or leave groupings/organisations—organisation may be functional or social

— obtain and use resources

— can define rules and regulations and enforce them in sub-areas of the 'real-world'

- Events occurring in the 'real-world' are monitored by a special agent called the real-world-environment-agent (RWEA). This agent knows the factual picture about everything that is happening in the real-world. It is responsible for managing events, making sure their consequences occur and then informing agents about them (simulating sensory feedback).

- By attaching stochastic, conditional and timed events to the RWEA, it is possible to test create tributary happenings in the real-world, thus testing the robustness of the agents and the procedures that they follow.

- Definition of performance metrics, to be used for collecting information about the quality and efficiency of the operations and the organisation of the agents.

During each simulation/modelling cycle, the user can set a number of parameters, for example:

- select classes and instances of objects that are to be modelled

- set values, or constrain the range of values, that the attributes of each selected object can take

- define various types of events and the pattern of their occurrence (e.g. stochastic functions)

- alter/define the beliefs of individual agents

- choose performance metrics to be collected

- view the world from the point of view of individual agents

- monitor the messages that are exchanged between agents

- change the way agents are organised and the procedures that they follow

How does an agent work?

Figure 1 shows the general structure of a CADDIE agent. Each agent can communicate with other agents via one or more communications media. Each agent has a knowledge-base consisting of non-executable (i.e. what it knows about itself and the world) and executable (i.e. how to perform tasks) knowledge.

Messages received from other agents and the internal knowledge-base of the agent determine what an agent does, when and how.

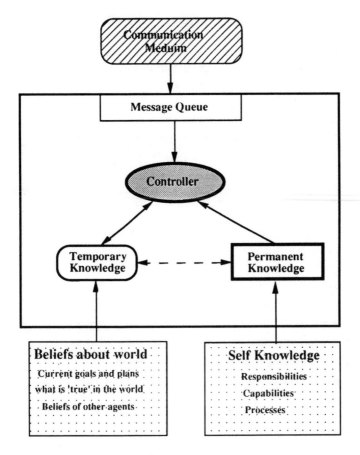

Figure 1 Internal structure of CADDIE agents.

The controller within each agent is responsible for the following activities:

- maintaining a prioritised task agenda (jobs to be done)
- arranging for execution and monitoring of actions
- processing messages received from other agents.

How is an organisation modelled in CADDIE?

CADDIE's agent-based approach to modelling organisations is based on a concept called the Functional UNit (FUN) [Farhoodi et al 91, Farhoodi

93] which is its basic data structure for building complex models of organisations. From a conceptual point of view a FUN is a schema which describes the attributes of each of the functional components of an organisation. Examples of these attributes include:

- its goals and objectives
- its policy, including organisational procedures
- its strategy, including current plans for achieving objectives.

From a more computational viewpoint the above attributes can be decomposed and categorised into static (those which always hold for a FUN throughout any experimentation run) and dynamic (those which may vary in an experimentation run).

The Functional Unit representation provides a flexible framework for experimentation with:

- different styles of organisation
- dynamic and static structures
- the relationship between social and functional organisation
- relationships between organisations and the environment
- different communication and control strategies
- alternative topology designs.

Performance measurement

The performance evaluation model in CADDIE consists of two main components, a set of control variables and a set of metrics. Control variables are decision variables which, if altered, produce changes in associated performance measures or metrics. Both control variables and performance metrics are envisaged to have the following dimensions:

- level of granularity (micro—agent level and macro—over a set of agents)
- epistemology (computational, generic organisational theory, domain specific).

The metrics utilised in CADDIE can be defined in terms of both effectiveness (ability to achieve a stated objective) and efficiency (ability to maximise output from given input or resources—these may include time, human resources, physical/hardware resources etc.).

Support for defining the following categories of metrics is provided:

- computational (e.g. communication load)
- generic organisational (e.g. flexibility)
- application or domain specific (e.g. environmental damage due to spillage of a chemical)

Further examples of organisational metrics that can be supported include:

- operational flexibility
- inter-operability
- resource availability
- survivability
- operational efficiency.

EXAMPLE APPLICATION

This section describes an example application from the domain of Emergency Services Command & Control. This example revolves around a tanker that has spilled its chemicals on an urban road, and the management of this incident by police and fire brigade services (see Figure 2).

The objective of this scenario is to evaluate the current procedures of the police and the fire brigade and explore alternative strategies for cooperation among police units and between the police and the fire service, in the context of a hypothetical incident.

Application specific metrics used in this scenario include:

- extent of environmental damage caused by chemical pollution
- time taken to restore the incident situation to normal.

Scenario scope

The scope of this scenario was limited to the study of:

- consequences of communication breakdowns, for example, because of:
  — unavailability of adequate communication resources
  — non-communication of agents due to overload, e.g. an agent receiving too much information which they cannot handle, i.e. cognitive overload

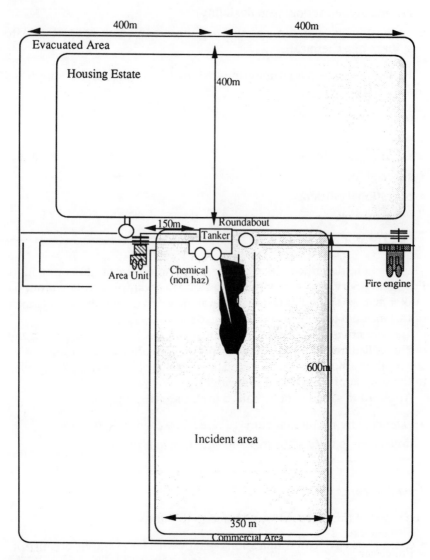

Figure 2 Emergency services scenario starting point.

- effects of alternative co-ordination regimes, between the police and the fire service, e.g.:
  - co-ordination by hierarchical partnership (i.e. police in overall charge)
  - co-ordination by co-operative ephemeral partnership (e.g. exchanging plans etc.)
- impact of varying distribution of authority and responsibility on the efficiency with which organisational objectives are achieved
- results of changes to operational procedures

FUNs

- 999 control room—999_FUN
- Police control room—Police_FUN
- Fire task unit(s)—Fire_FUN
- Senior on scene (bronze police unit)—Senior_on_scene_FUN
- Area (police) unit & equipment—Area_unit_FUN

Problem solving agents

- 999 control room operator
- Police control room operator
- Chief fire officer
- Fireman
- Chief Inspector/Inspector
- Police Constables

Other objects

- Communications facilities
- Fire engine
- Police car
- Fire appliances
- Life saving equipment
- Auxiliary equipment, e.g. accident signs

Strategic objectives

The overall objective of the emergency services is to maintain a safe environment and where necessary, to restore an abnormal situation to normality.

Each of the emergency services will have their own specific objectives and criteria but their main strategic objectives can be summed up as follows:

  (i) protect life and well-being

 (ii) protect property

(iii) restore normality

Corrective goals

Any violation of the strategic objectives must, by definition, be dealt with according to the priorities as listed below, e.g.:

Goal	Processes involved
life	evacuate_area, cordon_off_area, divert_traffic
fire	extinguish_fire
chemical	neutralise_chemical
unexploded bomb	neutralise_bomb
offence	prevent or stop offence

Tasks/processes

All FUNs in the emergency services scenario can perform the following tasks:

forward_message
receive_message
send_message
supply_information
add_information

update_information
retract_information
process_job_application
offer_job
deny_job
employ_agent
dismiss_agent

These tasks/capabilities can be given to the agents within each FUN:

join_FUN
leave_FUN
update_FUN_records
assemble_unit
   get all members and resources of the unit into one physical location
dispatch_unit
   unit (fully assembled or otherwise) to go to new physical location
assess_incident
   amalgamate as much information/data available about incident and
   utilise for outlining plans and tasks
prioritise_tasks
   prioritise chosen tasks
allocate_tasks
   allocate as current resourcing permits
request_backup
   at a number of points during the incident scenario (probably after
   assess_incident task) further units may be required
drive
   ability to drive a road vehicle

Events

Examples of types of events that can occur in this scenario include:

- Random (stochastic)—e.g. random resource breakdowns
- Time-scheduled—e.g. incident_occurred
- Conditional—e.g. incident_information_received_by_police

Communication and co-ordination

Examples of types of communications in the scenario include:

inform;
request_information;

acknowledge	(message received);
instruction_to_execute	(tell an agent what to do);
accept	(accept instruction and execute);
conditional_accept	(accept instruction with conditions and only execute task when conditions are met);
reject	(reject instruction).

Scenario execution

The scenario starts by the arrival of a 999 call at the police control centre, that a tanker has overturned and spilled some chemicals. The control centre then broadcasts a message to all police units under its control, asking them to respond with their position and availability. Each police car that receives this communication sends a reply back to the control centre. The control centre evaluates each reply based on proximity to the incident. It then requests the nearest unit to go to the scene of the incident. On arrival, the first police unit assesses the severity of the incident and then requests backup if necessary. A second police unit containing a senior officer is then dispatched to the incident, as well as a fire brigade unit (see Figure 3). On arrival, the senior officer receives a briefing and then assumes command. The senior_on_scene_FUN dynamically expands and will now have two extra members from the first unit (see Figure 4). On joining the senior FUN the first two police officers gain access to the senior units' resources (e.g. traffic cones) and proceed to position them around the incident area. The fire brigade unit arrives and it also becomes under the command of the senior police unit. The fire brigade is equipped with a hose and chemical dispersing material. The chemical spillage is washed off and all units return to base.

Example experiments:

- trying out alternative communication styles between the 999 control centre and the emergency services (e.g. maintaining a capability profile of each unit and using selective communication instead of broadcasting)
- stochastic corruption of messages, to study how the existing procedures cope with communication failures. For example, adding a new

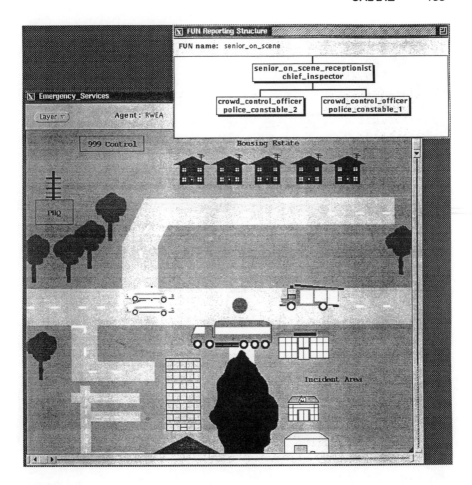

Figure 3

procedure which requires re-transmission of messages could reduce the chances of a unit getting lost, due to the corruption of the first transmission of the message specifying the location of the incident

- the fire brigade and police units maintaining their separate command structures and then cooperating through negotiation

- the fire brigade not having the appropriate equipment and having to use substitutes or returning to base to re-equip

- crowd management problems

- explosion of the tanker

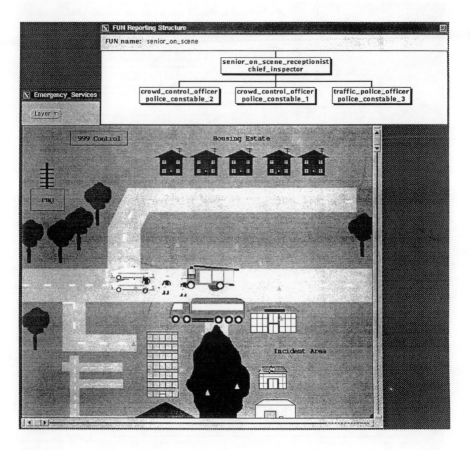

Figure 4

CONCLUSION

In order for an enterprise to succeed, its managers need to be able to effectively model various aspects of its operations, structure and environment. Process modelling, although useful, is not by itself sufficient to fulfil this need, given the complexities of modern businesses and their interactions with the environment.

This paper has described CADDIE, which is a new generation of advanced AI-based tool, which can support sophisticated business modelling at both macro and micro levels.

CADDIE's object-oriented approach builds on some of the latest work in the fields of AI and organisational theory, to provide a rich integrated framework for the representation of business processes, organisational knowledge and specification of performance metrics.

REFERENCES

Farhoodi, F., Proffitt, J., Woodman, P., Tunnicliffe, A. 1991. "An approach to the modelling of functional organisation". In Proceedings of the 10th UK Planning SIG.

Farhoodi, F., Proffitt, J., Woodman, P., Tunnicliffe, A. 1991. "Design of organisations in distributed decision systems". In Proceedings of the Workshop on Cooperation Among Heterogeneous Intelligent Agents, AAAI.

Farhoodi, F. 1993. "An approach to the explicit modelling of organisations and performance measurement". IEE Colloquium on Enterprise Modelling.

Galbraith, J. 1988. "Organisational Design", Addison-Wesley.

Morgan, G. 1984. "Creative Organisation Theory", Heinemann, London.

9

The Development Environment for Business Process Re-Engineering

Chris Moss

INTRODUCTION

Business Process Re-engineering is currently one of the hot topics for both the business and IT communities. Most organisations seem to be at least interested in the subject, tempted by the enormous benefits claimed by the advocates of the approach. Indeed, which organisation would not welcome the opportunity to rework, with the benefit of hindsight, processes, organisational structures and IT systems which have grown up over time? Less, however, is heard about the inherent risks of Business Process Re-engineering and how to reduce the likelihood of failure.

Before going any further, it is necessary to define **Business Process Re-Engineering.** Business Process Re-Engineering, or BPR, is a business driven, top-down investigation and redesign of business processes and objectives. The business is reworked to improve effectiveness in meeting key objectives, such as customer focus, and efficiency in

Software Assistance for Business Re-engineering. Edited by Kathy Spurr, Paul Layzell, Leslie Jennison and Neil Richards
© 1993 John Wiley & Sons Ltd

meeting those objectives. Following acceptance of the initial BPR project's recommendations, a series of reorganisation and IT projects are required to actually rework the business.

Before proceeding further, it must be emphasised that BPR should not be confused with IT strategy, or Information Systems Planning (ISP) exercises. IT strategy exercises are distinct from BPR in scope and in drivers. In ISP style projects, the remit to change business practices is in practice often limited to fine tuning within existing organisational boundaries. IT strategy exercises are often driven by the IT department, certainly in practice if not formally.

Since implementing BPR usually requires reorganisation of the business and large changes in the role and culture of employees, the costs of implementing inappropriate BPR recommendations are extremely high. One of the best methods of reducing this risk is to ensure that the initial BPR project is well thought out before inception and properly supported throughout. What is needed, in fact, is a well-designed environment within which the BPR project can take place. It is this environment which is the subject of this paper. There is an abundance of material available on BPR itself; an initial reference is provided at the end of this paper [1].

The **development environment** is the framework within which a project takes place. It can be seen as the project infrastructure. A development environment has three main components. Firstly there is a set of human and organisational considerations. This area, although a little vague in scope, is of critical importance. The second component is the activities, or processes, performed during the project. The development environment must define what these activities are and what procedures are used to perform them. The final component is the set of tools providing support for people performing these activities. If this definition is considered for a moment, it leads to the point that the development environment exists whether or not it is designed and controlled—there will always be people and an organisational structure, activities to perform, and tools used to perform them. The development environment is, in effect, a fact of life.

Given tight deadlines and limited resources, the task of designing a development environment may seem to be an overhead to a BPR project, and one of dubious returns at that. The key justifications for investing in establishing a suitable environment are firstly, that the environment exists whether it is designed or not, and should be optimised; secondly, that given the business critical nature of BPR the investment in a sound environment is likely to be justified; and finally, that the exercise of establishing the environment is a useful learning experience to feed into the BPR project itself.

To balance the equation, the costs of implementing a development environment must be considered. The main costs are:

- effort spent designing the development environment;
- purchasing tools;
- customising tools;
- purchasing equipment;
- training staff.

It should be noted that some of these costs will be experienced whether or not the development environment is explicitly designed. The most cost effective implementation may be to extend an existing IT systems development environment, as some procedures and tools are likely to be in place already.

Having discussed the justification for designing a BPR environment, the individual components of that environment will be investigated. As mentioned above, these are the human issues to be addressed; activities to be performed; and the toolset to support the above.

Each of these areas is explored in more detail below.

HUMAN ISSUES

The human area of any development environment is critical, whatever the activities being supported by the environment. However, many discussions on infrastructure and project environments seem to neglect or ignore this area. The importance of getting the human issues right is especially paramount in BPR, where there is less structure and more need for creativity than in, say, a systems development environment.

One of the key issues in this area is visible management backing. Senior management must be committed to the project; furthermore, they must be seen to be committed by the rest of the organisation—it's not sufficient that only the BPR project leader knows that senior management is behind the project. Strong, publicly-announced commitment from the highest level ensures the BPR team know their findings will be acted upon; further, by adding to the credibility of the BPR project, fuller co-operation from the rest of the organisation is likely.

Another key area is selection of team members; BPR projects are often small enough to allow careful consideration of team membership. A typical BPR project might consist of 15 to 25 people.

In terms of staffing a BPR project, a good mix of people is essential. Staff with experience of all areas within the scope of the project should either be on the project or be accessible to it. It is important, within this, to distinguish between levels of experience; both strategic and detailed knowledge is needed, which may entail different people. For those readers familiar with Joint Application Development terminology, these levels of knowledge equate roughly with 'decision takers' and 'knowledge workers'.

Another important staffing consideration is the blend of personalities. It's probably not a good idea, for example, to staff the project entirely with creative intellectuals as the project may become unfocused. A mix of personalities is the best policy, including people who will push the project through and those who will finish the job. The Belbin team roles model could be used in building the team—see reference [2].

The use of part-time staff for some of the team should be explored; part-time staff may suffer distractions from the project but provide an anchor in the real business world and ensure continuous visibility for the project in the business as a whole. External consultants are often used on BPR projects. External consultants can provide experience of BPR and can a give a fresh view of the business. They can also, through their experience, dominate the project. Further, if a group of consultants has performed many BPR projects, especially in the same market sector, they may find it difficult to break away from solutions more appropriate to earlier clients. A final point is that staff assigned to long term BPR projects, e.g. in excess of 6 months, can experience stress and distractions as to what job they will return to after the BPR project ends.

The organisation of the project team also needs consideration. Generally, the organisation needs to be flexible with the ability to form multidisciplinary subgroups. One approach is to divide the project team along existing organisational boundaries. This has obvious drawbacks for a project which is intended to overcome existing boundaries, in particular by impeding radical thinking and reinforcing interdepartmental politics. Such a structure is, however, easy to understand, and lets the project get started. It can always be amended later in the project.

Another approach is to divide the project into subteams to perform each BPR activity, as described later. This approach can be difficult to get to grips with, and may lead to domination of the project by 'gurus' in the BPR activities. It also runs counter to the integration of BPR activities. The importance of integrated activities is discussed below. This approach is perhaps best limited to creation of a few specialist functions, e.g. the application of certain BPR techniques.

The final approach is to organise the project team by business topics, identified in the early stages of the BPR project. This organisation can be confusing and may need to change as issues change. It may be best applied as an evolution from organising the team along existing organisational boundaries, but represents an overhead in management and communication as the structure changes. It may also be harder to communicate the structure outside the project, should this become necessary.

A good physical working environment is also important; however, this less than glamorous aspect of the development environment often gets neglected. Requirements must be borne in mind for a number of areas, including adequate desks and PC's, etc.; lots of meeting areas for brainstorming and meetings; proximity to information providers; and availability of technical support.

A final point in the human and organisational issues area is to run only one BPR project at a time. There are examples of organisations running multiple BPR-type projects at once, especially where not all exercises bear the BPR label. This reduces both the internal and external credibility of the BPR project and makes analysis more complex, as it is based upon a shifting organisation. The only exception to this rule should be if multiple BPR projects are taking place within tightly scoped and exclusive areas— effectively organisations within their own right.

ACTIVITIES WITHIN A BPR PROJECT

Having considered the human issues of a BPR project, we can consider the activities to be performed within the project. There are a number of areas of activity in a BPR project; the most important point is to consider all of the areas of activity. The main areas are:

- management of project activities;
- production of BPR deliverables;
- management of quality;
- management of BPR deliverables.

Project management in BPR projects involves the standard activities of identifying and planning for all tasks, deliverables and resources, then monitoring actual progress against the plan, and addressing slippages and problems as they arise. Some of the particular project management challenges with BPR are handling new issues as the BPR identifies them and keeping the project within budget as new areas of interest arise.

Production of BPR deliverables and working documents is often driven by a BPR methodology or techniques set. Rather than, in effect, develop their own methodology, most organisations consider using an 'off the shelf' methodology. This has the advantage of having many of the required elements already in place, and should be tried and tested. Methodologies are, however, produced to be generic, in order to reach as wide a market as possible. As a result, it is worth considering tailoring any methodology selected, for a number of reasons: the techniques may not be applicable to the organisation, e.g. in some organisations rule based processing is a key requirement; the methodology may be limited in scope; the methodology may have weak areas; the lifecycle may be too restrictive; the methodology may not cover project management, quality management and management of deliverables; some of the above areas may be covered, but in a way that conflicts with preferred, existing practices.

The techniques to be used to produce the BPR deliverables is a key decision and often, regrettably, the major component of a methodology. One of the factors which can get neglected when assessing techniques is the acceptability of the techniques and their deliverables to the project team and to reviewers. The learning curve involved in becoming adept in the techniques is also important, especially as they may be used on only one BPR project.

The techniques' track record should be investigated. A final point is that complex techniques can distract team members from solving the real business problems; in struggling to master the concepts and notation of a particular technique, thinking about the underlying business problem can be neglected. The technique then becomes an end in its own right rather than just a means to an end.

The key point to be made with respect to techniques is, however, that techniques are only one component of the BPR development environment. It is not uncommon to concentrate only on the techniques at the expense of other areas of activity listed above. Experience of using IT structured techniques methods shows that in such an environment, the potential benefits will be realised to a limited extent.

As well as producing the BPR deliverables, the development environment must address managing the quality of these deliverables. Given the consequences of producing an inappropriate set of BPR deliverables, quality management is even more important in BPR than in many other disciplines. Quality in BPR should be focused on ensuring that the deliverables identify and describe all of the business issues and provide a complete set of recommendations. The 'tick in the box' type of quality criteria (e.g. all properties documented) which are important in other fields are relatively less important in BPR. The important quality criterion for BPR deliverables is that the deliverable must capture the business accurately. This is subjective and best enforced through walkthroughs with business staff. All the standard quality management activities must be thought through and applied: quality criteria must be identified for all BPR deliverables; quality assurance measures and deliverables must be selected; quality activities must be built into the project plan.

The final major area of activity is management of BPR deliverables and working documents. The actual products vary with the methodology used, but might typically include models and definitions of current processes and of redesigned processes, migration plans for moving to the new processes, implications for the existing organisational structure and staff grades, cost benefit analyses, IT implications, project plans, reports, sign-off documents, interview notes, roles and responsibility matrices and process to location matrices.

All these product results should be centrally available, if different team members are to use them. It should be possible for team members to reuse existing products, e.g. process definitions, rather than invent their own. The outline list of deliverables shows that a lot of textual data must be managed, e.g. reports, interview notes, etc., in addition to diagrams and structured data.These are often neglected in development environments; there is as strong a requirement that these are centrally available as for techniques-based deliverables.

As deliverables are signed off, it will be necessary to implement change control procedures for them. The management of deliverables should be resolved before the project commences; if not, problems in this area have a habit of making themselves known when the project is underway, typically at the worst possible moment.

The environment must allow for the passing on and reuse of deliverables in subsequent business and IT projects, to avoid duplication of effort and to ensure the BPR is followed through properly. This area is one where automation has a key role to play, as will be discussed in the tools section.

Having identified and discussed the activities in the BPR project, it is worth noting that the low level tasks stemming from these activities should be integrated with one another. This is because activities will be more effective if integrated—quality assurance in particular is more likely to be successful if it is viewed by team members as an integral part of the process; otherwise it can be seen as an overhead, probably optional and the first area to be cut if timescales are tight. Resistance to activities other than just producing deliverables will be reduced if they are integral to the project. The same issues are true of project management and of managing data. Further, integration of activities improves productivity, as the integration of activities helps remove duplication of effort. Finally consistency between deliverables is more likely to be achieved if activities are integrated, rather than if groups work in isolation, as they should be working on the same data.

Actual integration of activities is achieved by combining them into a project lifecycle. The lifecycle may be built from scratch or else may take a methodology's lifecycle as a starting point, then be amended. The core of the lifecycle will come from the activities which generate the BPR deliverables. Further activities must then be added and existing activities amended to cater for project management, quality management and management of deliverables.

THE TOOLSET FOR BPR

The toolset is the final component of a BPR development environment, after human issues and activities.

The toolset should support all of the activities to be performed. The key word in this requirement is *all*, i.e. it's not sufficient that just techniques are supported while project management and deliverables management are neglected. It is very likely that more than one tool will be needed.

The tool(s) you select should support your ways of working, rather than imposing unwanted changes in practice. This implies that flexible tools are preferable. There are other ways you may wish to adapt the tool, e.g. to manage a tailored BPR lifecycle and to store deliverables specific to your organisation (transport and insurance firms, for example, may need to analyse some areas of their business unique to their market sector). Tools which are customisable are therefore important.

Usability is also a key issue, as most BPR team members will not be used to using tools of this nature. If a mix of tools are used, as far as possible they should share an interface or have common interface standards, e.g. run under the same PC operating system and have the same 'look and feel'.

The tool should support reuse of deliverables within the project: otherwise team members will create their own data rather than reuse existing definitions. This leads to wasted effort, inconsistency within the project and poor communication. To support reuse, the tool must allow users to find existing definitions in an unstructured fashion, e.g. by specifying some properties of the deliverable required. This is achieved by storing deliverables within a central repository, which supports links between deliverables and allows user queries based on properties of the data.

The toolset should also support the passing on of deliverables to business and IT projects spawned from the BPR project. These projects will need to be able to use the BPR deliverables as a starting point. It may also be necessary to pass deliverables refined by projects back to the BPR deliverables, in order to maintain the BPR deliverables as a correct view of the business.

One implication of the above points is that subsequent business and IT projects should ideally use the same toolset as the initial BPR. This point should be borne in mind when selecting a toolset; flexibility and extensibility of the toolset become key requirements.

In order to support integrated activities, an integrated toolset is required. It is difficult to integrate activities which use different tools. All tools in the toolset should share the same data definitions, to support reuse.

One approach to providing a toolset is to base it on separate tools and to build interfaces between them. This allows 'best of breed' tools to be selected and may allow existing tools to be built into the toolset. However, as data is passed between tools, rather than the data actually being shared, different versions of data arise which must be reconciled and cause conflict communication problems. Also, interfaces between the tools must be built and maintained, in particular when different tools are upgraded by the vendors. Control of the environment falls back on manual controls, e.g. the initiation of file transfers between tools. A usability issue also arises, in so much as the tools may not share a common interface or even run on the same workstations.

Another approach is to use a single tool which supports all required activities. Data is then shared by all parts of the tool, avoiding problems with conflicting data definitions. Users are confident they are accessing the latest version of data. Quality assurance is also easier as reviewers can be granted direct access to deliverables at all times. The problem here is that no one tool is likely to support all your activities. Alternatively, the tool may provide support which is not as good as the best available tool (the 'best of breed') for that area. An approach to this problem is to select a tool with coverage in most areas, then customise it, including adding interfaces to additional tools if necessary. An excellent solution is to adapt and extend a toolset, and activities, already in place for a systems development environment. This saves money and time, and has the advantage that much of the environment will already be in place.

Ideally, tools from different vendors would share a repository and a user interface, supporting both 'best of breed' tools, on the one hand, and shared data and a common user interface, on the other. For this approach to work, not only must the technical issues of physical tool integration be resolved, but different tools must be able to share the same underlying model of shared data. This latter problem may prove to be the harder to solve.

CONCLUSIONS

Having considered the human, procedural and tool components of a development environment, it is worth discussing a few conclusions. Firstly, given the magnitude of the benefits and risks incumbent in BPR, it seems it is worth expending some effort, and hard cash, on setting up a development environment which does everything practical to ensure the success and quality of the project and its deliverables.

When designing the environment, it is necessary to look at the whole picture; it is not sufficient to take an existing methodology with a technique support tool and then expect these to meet a BPR project's needs. Customising and reusing an environment already in place for systems development is a good option as time and money are saved.

When looking at the human aspects of the environment, choosing and optimising your team is a key factor in achieving success. Several factors need to be considered, including the background and personalities of the team members. The project must be backed up by visible, senior management commitment.

With respect to activities, it is essential that management and administration type activities, i.e. project management, quality management and management of deliverables, are not neglected in favour of just producing deliverables. Starting the project without putting in place a proper framework for these areas will lead to higher costs and disruption later in the project.

Another conclusion is that customisation of methods and tools is usually required, as it is unlikely that 'off the shelf' solutions will meet all requirements. The environment should be integrated—activities should be integrated via the lifecycle and the toolset should share data using an integrated repository.

Further, the toolset and methodology should encourage and entrench reuse of deliverables; one of the key tools in achieving this is a repository which supports browsing and unstructured access to deliverables.

The final conclusion is that the development environment put in place for BPR should be used for the follow-on projects. Or, as there may already be a development environment in place for other projects, perhaps this environment should be amended for BPR ?

Chris Moss is a senior consultant with Softlab Ltd. Softlab produce and market Maestro, an Integrated-CASE tool with strong process management and configuration management capabilities. As part of assisting Maestro sites, Softlab provide consultancy on development environments for Systems Development and, more recently, for Business Process Re-Engineering. This experience is drawn upon in this paper.

REFERENCES

[1] Business Change and Re-engineering (Journal) Publishers: Cornwallis Emmanuel
[2] Management Teams, R.M.Belbin, 1981 Publishers: Heinemann

Section 3

How Can We Make Business Re-Engineering Work?

Kathy Spurr

I do not ... want to give the impression that the use of large machines or of elaborate techniques is always justified; sometimes it contributes merely to the sense of self-importance of the investigator, and it is always salutory to remember Rutherford's 'We haven't got the money, so we've got to think!'

R.V. Jones quoting Ernest Rutherford (1871–1937), in Bulletin of the Institute of Physics (1962) vol 13, p 102

The seminar having addressed methods and tools for Business Re-engineering, the two speakers for this session were faced with the difficult task of pulling all this together and answering the pertinent question, "How can we make Business Re-Engineering work?".

Both speakers drew from their experience of international consultancy in the area of business re-engineering, and both highlighted the importance of customer values. The presentations differed in that Michael Mills felt that software tools can actively help business re-engineering, whereas Linda Hickman urged caution, believing that the formulation of a model for such a tool may oversimplify the business essentials, and disguise crucial factors.

Software Assistance for Business Re-engineering. Edited by Kathy Spurr, Paul Layzell, Leslie Jennison and Neil Richards
© 1993 John Wiley & Sons Ltd

Michael Mills discussed his experiences of business re-engineering and his use of the Business Design Facility (BDF). This has been used internally within Texas Instruments and with some client sites around the world. He used an example of changes made to an order management system within Texas Instruments.

Mills believes that value judgements are important for business re-engineering. This is a theme which has been echoed by other speakers during the seminar. He expressed concern about the "flat view" of the organisation portrayed by diagrams such as entity-relationship and data flow diagrams. For business re-engineering, customer values are important. Mills reiterated that traditional CASE tools have limited applicability for business re-engineering, since they are designed for a different purpose: namely to design software rather than to re-engineer a business. The BDF is not a CASE tool, since it is able to store customer value judgements.

Mills discussed features within a business which may indicate that the internal process could be reorganised more effectively. Internal telephones were used as an example. These are often used to chase up errors; for example "Where is that order"? If you could prevent the error occurring in the first place through better business engineering, then much of the need for internal communications may disappear, freeing the people in the business for more valuable work. Mills seemed to imply that businesses may be more effective if the internal telephone system were abolished: a revolutionary idea which might give us all cause for thought! He stated that the role of people within a business should be to make things happen— not to do the work! "The work" can often be done more effectively using automation.

Any method or tool for business re-engineering should help identify areas where there is confusion within the business. To illustrate the confusion which can arise within large business organisations, Mills used an example of a process "Set Stock Level" within a major company. Various personnel within the business, from senior managers to order clerks, have some say in the process, but it is not clear who actually has responsibility for it.

Linda Hickman continued the theme of the importance of customer values. She disposed rapidly of the "alphabet soup" of terms used for business re-engineering (BPR, BPE, BE, . . .) claiming that these can cloud the real issue which is concerned with the business perspective. She stated that "competitive advantage is the reason that we are all in business— but technology and Information Technology (IT) departments have failed proactively to provide this competitive advantage".

Value chain analysis is a business technique which helps to build richer models of the business. It helps identify areas where IT can improve the business process since each of the value activities has an information component. Value chain analysis is important for business re-engineering. This mechanism examines customer values and how they are supported by existing business processes. Customer values must have a priority in any business re-engineering activity.

Hickman highlighted the divide between the IT department and the business: IT practitioners are concerned with representing sufficient detail in a model, but this model fails the business for two reasons:

(i) Normally, the model is static rather than dynamic, which limits its applicability for modelling a dynamic business environment.

(ii) The IT model has been constructed for use by IT practitioners and so reflects IT values rather than business values.

Hickman presented a clear account of mainstream business re-engineering, giving us a rapid tour of its characteristics and the business pressures which are driving its use. Read this paper for a perspective on the importance of benchmarking, and the need to understand the model's dynamic complexity. (In the previous section, Faramarz Farhoodi gave an account of current work on exactly this frontier.)

Linda Hickman warns us of the limitations of simple static models, but she is not against the use of tools. She reminds us that business re-engineering is a process itself, which can benefit from the use of integrated tools. Linda Hickman sees a common repository as key to integration, while Michael Mills described some of the additional possibilities of desktop interworking between tools.

Both speakers identified the important differences between the IT approach to building information systems, based upon detail, and the business re-engineering approach to improving business performance based on value analysis of dynamic business processes. Michael Mills saw business re-engineering supported by tools, while Linda Hickman urged caution in this area.

During the seminar, in general, we saw advocacy and evidence for each of these views. Some felt that the jury was still out. No doubt, in the future, we shall be hearing many more accounts of experience, and there will be further developments in the area of software assistance for business re-engineering. As we accumulate this evidence, we shall be able to build up our own view of the contribution that can be made to business re-engineering by appropriate tools.

10

Automating Business Process Re-Engineering with the Business Design Facility

Michael Mills, Clive Mabey

ABSTRACT

Texas Instruments (TI) has developed a software tool to support Business Process Re-engineering (BPR). In carrying out BPR, both external market forces and the organisation of the enterprise need to be examined, following key "Process Chains" that comprise the activities of multiple internal functions (departments) to achieve a complete result. Previous business improvement programmes have often been restricted to improving a single process within a limited organisational space. BPR, however, by focusing on cross-functional issues, is able to provide a much higher level of business process optimisation, resolving the sometimes conflicting goals of different departments.

BPR aims to improve the business by changing the rules and procedures, organisation and workflow. Because it involves changing the business, including the activities of both people and equipment, it requires human

Software Assistance for Business Re-engineering. Edited by Kathy Spurr, Paul Layzell,
Leslie Jennison and Neil Richards
© 1993 John Wiley & Sons Ltd

thought and management. As such, it can never be automated. However, it is possible to use computer tools to support the human thought required by BPR. Inevitably, a BPR project collects and correlates significant amounts of data, and simulates potential solutions: tasks for which an integrated software tool is useful to the BPR professional. Such a tool must use or interface with popular BPR facilities, including Activity-Based Costing analysis, spreadsheets, word processors and simulation packages.

In a re-engineered process solution, the process worker needs holistic computer support, providing access to all the data needed across a specific process chain. The traditional solution—rewriting existing departmental systems to achieve back-end integration around a database—is expensive, slow and problematic. A more timely solution, which lends itself to BPR projects, is Client/Server computing using front-end desktop integration (on the client workstation used by the case worker) and giving easy access to many separate existing systems, perhaps with heterogeneous server platforms.

OVERVIEW

As a leader in applying continuous quality improvement programmes to their own internal processes, Texas Instruments (TI) came to realise that while the resulting incremental gains in quality and productivity were worthwhile, together they did not supply the overall business benefits that were really being sought.

A review of business performance, including benchmarking (comparison with other companies), identified the need to drive down cycle times for major business processes. While each sub-process in itself was efficient, the overall time taken to satisfy a request was much too long. A combination of major changes in processes, followed by repeated tuning of the new processes (Continuous Process Improvement), has since led to significant improvements in customer service and business performance.

Typically, though not always, a major change implies discontinuity. Discontinuous change means bringing about major leaps in process performance, through the engineering or re-engineering of those processes. The agent of this discontinuous change is Business Process Re-Engineering (BPR); it is the means by which the major leaps in process performance can be identified and achieved. Our experience of many BPR projects has enabled us to evolve a simple but powerful approach to achieving substantial business improvements: the BPR methodology.

Any methodology for BPR must ensure the gathering and organisation of facts and requirements needed for re-engineering processes. But it must never discourage that vital spark, the creative leap of imagination which suggests a transformation of the present business process into a far more effective activity.

The four main phases of BPR are often described as:

- Planning and information gathering
- Formalisation and modelling of the "As Is" situation
- Simulation and evaluation of the "Should Be" scenarios
- Implementation of the solution

One problem with so many BPR projects is the collection and storage of raw data and the need to evaluate in detail any creative proposals. The growing proportion of administrative tasks on the project often threatens to overwhelm the outward-looking, business-oriented, opportunity-seeking aspects of BPR. We end up unable to see the wood for trees. Sometimes, BPR projects overdo this data collection. Too much detail rarely assists in identifying problem areas; it is only useful for the subsequent design of solutions for specific BPR initiatives.

A second problem is formalisation. BPR projects must have an approach to formalisation which will condense the data collected to ensure completeness and consistency across the entire project. It is bad enough to miss a key element in a BPR project; much worse to have identified the key element and then lost it in the paperwork.

A third problem is testing. It must be possible to test theories about improving the current situation. In other words, the effects of any proposed changes to processes recommended by the BPR project must be tested and simulated.

Given our success in creating software tools for planning, analysis, design and integration, such as the Integrated-CASE (I-CASE) tool which supports and simplifies the information systems development life cycle, TI looked to see if a tool could be developed oriented to the specific needs of the business process practitioner.

The requirements were that the tool should be easily usable by BPR specialists; it should enable visualisation of the business processes in a format acceptable to business management and it should support the four main phases of BPR. Finally, it should be of open design, supporting any BPR methodology and interfacing to other tools within standard operating system services.

This tool design goal has been achieved with the Business Design Facility (BDF). Released in 1993, it is in early use at customer sites around the world. Initial feedback is in line with the comments of trial users that the BDF enables consistency and promotes iterative goal-seeking.

This goal-seeking activity is a key element. It is not too difficult to imagine changes to a business process, but it is far more difficult to evaluate alternative solutions and identify risks and opportunities. The provision of powerful spreadsheet modelling techniques using visualisation familiar to BPR practitioners and business managers encourages confidence in the business re-engineering solutions proposed.

A major factor in the development of the BDF was understanding the differences between information systems development (which should always include some element of business process improvement) and BPR. While both projects are interested in data and processes, the interest is in quite different properties of each.

In BPR we are interested in the cycle time and added-value of a process, cross-functional process chains, and organisational issues. In Information Engineering or information systems development, we are concerned with data attributes, field length, elementary processes, logic, and so forth—quite different aspects from BPR. What is exciting has been our ability to link these two aspects.

Today, virtually any BPR solution will call for changes to the supporting application systems, often in quite fundamental ways. The BDF tool has been designed to feed results between the BPR project and Information Systems projects. So the results of a BPR initiative can be fed into an I-CASE tool, such as TI's Information Engineering Facility™ (IEF™), to provide the starting point for building or modifying information systems, and to enable rapid implementation of the BPR recommendations. Alternatively, where the existing business process structure has been completed in an I-CASE tool, this can be fed into the BDF as its starting point for a BPR project.

We are now entering the second generation of BPR support tools with the design of the next version of the BDF, so we may see extensions to the way in which processes are visualised and represented, goal-seeking, scenario management, and the identification of conflicting goals across different processes. Improvements are being driven not only from our ongoing R&D efforts but more importantly by feedback from early users who can see their ideas and experience being translated into tools used worldwide.

WHY REDESIGN BUSINESS PROCESSES?

Modern business is taking place against a background of unprecedented change. Large companies with household names are losing market share to small companies whose names were not known a decade ago.

Transactions which cross international boundaries are rising sharply and much financing and sourcing now takes place on a global basis. Demand for customised products is on the rise at the expense of traditional mass produced products. Cut-throat competition on price is giving way to long-term customer/supplier relationships and superlative quality is now expected. These changes are fuelled by constant innovations in information technology and they take place within a framework of extreme economic uncertainty.

The keys to competing in today's environment are quality, speed and flexibility. Product innovation needs to take place on a continuous basis with radical reductions in the design-to-manufacture time. Manufacturing cycle time must also be reduced as should order-to-delivery lead times. These performance improvements need to be matched by high quality. This will involve reducing failure rates not only in the basic product or service but elsewhere in the business such as the supply and distribution network. What this means is that companies must examine their business processes very closely to understand how the performance of those business processes can be optimised.

WHAT IS A BUSINESS PROCESS?

A business process is an activity which takes an input and transforms it into an output. Each process has a beginning and an end. The beginning may be a request or an event and the end will be the outcome implied by that request or event. Taking procurement as an example (see Figure 1), it begins with a request from manufacturing, let's say, for parts to be used in the manufacturing process. The process finishes when the transaction is complete; the parts have been delivered to the satisfaction of the customer (manufacturing).

Every major business comprises sub-processes which, in turn, can be decomposed. Attention has been focused on optimising these sub-processes rather than the overall process. BPR looks at a wide canvas: the

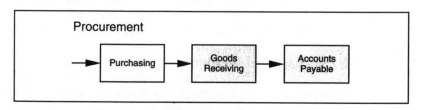

Figure 1   Example of a Procurement Process

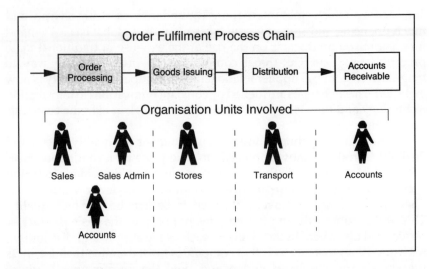

Figure 2   Order Fulfilment Process Chain

major business processes which are composed of a chain of sub-processes. Sub-processes tend to be small, and typically accumulations of such sub-processes are by organisation unit, as shown in Figure 2. However, BPR treats the accumulations of these sub-processes as taking place across functions; they form a "business process chain" which runs through the various organisation units. A business process chain is, therefore, a sequence of activities (processes) that achieve a business result. The chain is the process as seen by the customer, rather than the way in which sub-processes are grouped internally. For example, a customer who places an order is not concerned with the various sub-processes occurring within the organisation units which the order will pass through, but rather with the fulfilment of that order. The sub-processes which will fulfil that order are part of the business process chain and will cross functional boundaries.

In building information systems, the focus is on one or more low level processes; BPR, however, takes the holistic view. Though the discipline of focusing at the low level is still needed during implementation of a BPR solution, it is not needed during BPR analysis, where detail tends to obscure the picture.

In Figure 2, the Order Fulfilment Process Chain has a customer, who places the order, and that customer will have expectations of the process. These expectations can normally be expressed as measurable characteristics, for example, the time it takes from the moment the order is placed to the receipt of the goods ordered, the cost of the goods, or the number of defective goods. Understanding customer expectations of the process is essential to understanding how to optimise that process.

A business process chain will not, therefore, be performed physically by a single organisation unit or department within a business. In BPR, we need to be able to look at it in holistic fashion as it crosses functional boundaries. Optimising each component independently will not lead to an optimal solution.

The Ford Motor Company provides us with an excellent example of how the procurement process can be re-engineered to achieve superior performance. This example is quoted by Dr Michael Hammer (in the Harvard Business Review July/August 1990, "Reengineering Work, Don't Automate, Obliterate"). Ford felt that the cost of procurement was unduly high when compared with other motor manufacturers and set out to reduce that cost. Their initial idea was to lend automated support to the tasks that were currently being executed. This did not, however, lead to the improvements that were necessary to compare favourably with other companies. This is what Dr Hammer refers to as 'paving the cow paths' or automating existing processes rather than replacing them with new optimised processes.

It was only when Ford went back to the drawing board and decided to address the entire procurement process that the required performance improvements were found. The solution involved changing the business rules to ensure that only goods ordered were to be accepted by the receiving function and goods accepted were to be paid for automatically. Ford wrote to their suppliers and asked them not to send invoices.

The measures had the effect of reducing costs by about 75%. The reason for this was that most of the effort had been going into the reconciliation of what had been ordered, what had been received, and what had been invoiced. By changing the rules this reconciliation became unnecessary and the cost reductions followed.

TI'S ORDER FULFILMENT PROCESS

As a large high-tech corporation, TI suffered like many such enterprises with a static internal organisation while externally coping with rapidly changing products and markets. Realisation of the underlying problems led to a series of internal process re-engineering projects which are still continuing in various divisions. A typical example of a completed project covered the area of Order Fulfilment, as previously shown in Figure 2. The objective was to reduce order to manufacture times and improve on-time deliveries. Re-engineering work on the TI order fulfilment process was limited to those tasks comprising order processing, distribution, billing and payment. No attempt was made to re-engineer the manufacturing part of the process. The re-engineered solution is in place in some, but not all, of TI's businesses.

The BPR team adopted a holistic approach taking into account not only the internal functions involved but also the customers themselves. The results were quite sweeping. The solutions applied across a number of organisational units. Today, customers are online not only for purposes of placing orders but also for the purposes of payment which is done through EDI. TI aim to satisfy orders from finished goods inventory with the order taker empowered when manual intervention is necessary.

The management benefits are easily seen from the results metrics:

- Order entry cycle time improved by 30–68% depending on product range
- Staff reassigned amounted to 30–50%
- Shipping errors were reduced by 67–90%
- On-time delivery was improved from 88% to 93%
- Field queries were reduced by 60%

These results speak for themselves. It is important to note that all three key criteria of cycle time, cost and quality were improved. Indeed three separate measures of quality of the order fulfilment process itself showed improvement.

WHAT IS BUSINESS PROCESS RE-ENGINEERING?

BPR is an approach to optimising business performance which seeks radical change and major benefits. It challenges prior rules and assumptions; and probably calls on techniques from several disciplines. It frequently requires changes in jobs, organisations and reward systems. The objectives which drive this change must come from the business itself.

The visioning process which establishes the objectives is therefore a very important part of the BPR effort. For example, if like some retail organisations you are planning to make your suppliers responsible for getting their products onto the shelf, you won't want to look at current procurement processes in depth. It is therefore important that the visioning process starts with a clean slate and challenges any prior rules and assumptions, however long-lived and however cherished they might be.

By definition, a radical change in performance will imply a radical change in how things are done. This means that people must be prepared to do different jobs, perhaps in different organisational units, and it may even be necessary to change incentive schemes to ensure that people are properly motivated to perform their new tasks.

In this headlong dash to optimise business performance, questions often arise as to the role of Information Technology (IT). It is often asserted that IT has little to do with BPR. To examine this assertion it is helpful to consider BPR from two points of view: doing the right thing and doing things right.

Doing the right thing depends largely on industry knowledge, experience and intuition in circumstances where precise data is often difficult to come by. Despite this, IT is often the enabler as illustrated by well-known BPR successes such as Merrill Lynch's Cash Management Account, First Boston's home mortgage scheme and Walmart's desire to be in the business of renting shelves.

However, to radically improve process performance (do things right), IT is indispensable. Doing things right is concerned with the optimisation of repeatable processes which cross functional boundaries. It is at these boundaries that the real opportunities for performance improvement exist since historically most effort has gone into optimising the individual functional components rather than in making these components work effectively together. This means that a holistic approach must be adopted—the whole being more than the sum of the parts.

Business processes lend themselves to examination by analytic techniques such as business modelling. Effectively re-engineered business processes are characterised by the existence of metrics which measure the efficiency and effectiveness of the process and which motivate Continuous Process Improvement thereafter. These measurements, which are performance-oriented, such as cycle-time, cost and quality, can be profoundly affected by the way information is managed within the process.

For example, to return to the re-engineering example of the Order Fulfilment process, a number of possible metrics exist against which order fulfilment can be measured. The ones actually chosen will be determined by the procedures employed and the availability of accurate and up-to-date information.

A typical list might include:

- Lead times compared to competitors
- Percentage of on-time orders
- Time to respond to customer inquiries
- Number of orders delivered incorrectly
- Number of queries from the field
- Cost of dealing with returns
- Effort expended per order

The set of metrics clearly depends on the characteristics of the process chain and the goals of the business. The BDF enables practitioners to identify any number of different metrics which can be stored, accumulated or simulated.

HOW CAN INFORMATION TECHNOLOGY HELP?

IT can ensure the instant availability of correct and up-to-date information simultaneously to every part of a business process. It can completely replace certain tasks such as verification against specified rules and can substantially improve the efficiency of remaining manual tasks. Key opportunities which need to be exploited include faster and broader access to information, improved correctness/consistency of information, improved currency of information with the elimination of physical flows of information as well as the automation of manual tasks.

BPR re-emphasises the key role of data sharing across departments and product lines, for example, the need for banks to have one image of a customer rather than several images of a customer based on the number of accounts they hold. IT is able to achieve this data sharing by providing information through on-line access to database technology. Information, once created, is instantly available to all other users who are allowed access. This eliminates the need for paper and other physical flows of information. It also reduces the need for copying information manually between documents, for example, orders and delivery notes, and in so doing eliminates a major cause of errors. While many of these points may seem obvious to IT professionals, common business practice still enshrines many such manual tasks. Together the elimination of the creation, transportation and replication of information leads to considerable effort saving.

In addition consistency and currency are achievable by presenting a single image of information to all functions even when the information is stored redundantly. By eliminating physical flows of information we are able to reduce propagation time, reduce transcription errors, control data redundancy, and improve both consistency and currency.

In many enterprises today IT has been successfully applied at the departmental or functional level. Islands of automation exist within functional areas but communication between them is still achieved by physical flows of information (see Figure 3). This has a negative effect on cycle time, cost and quality. It also means that while department managers may have access to information about their individual functions, often there is the *business issue* that no one person is responsible for the performance of the business process chain (a process owner). Even where

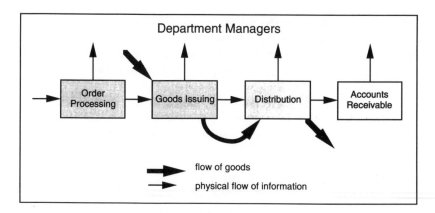

Figure 3 IT has tended to concentrate on information flows; BPR also considers physical flows between functional areas

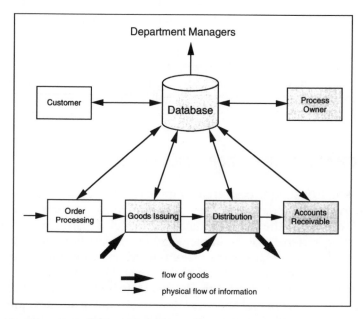

Figure 4 Data consolidated throughout the business process

a process owner does exist, there is the *IT issue* that frequently adequate and consistent data across the chain is not easily available.

One approach might be to consolidate all the data required throughout the business process into a single database and eliminate the physical flows (see Figure 4). This would have an important extra benefit, namely to make available information on the whole process. It would even be possible to appoint a manager for the process as IBM Credit did for their credit checking process with dramatic effects on cycle time (see later example). We might also choose to integrate suppliers and customers into the process as TI has done.

The feasibility of this approach depends critically on two things: the logistics and the cost of implementing the change. Given the scope of the changes (an entire process) these issues take on considerable weight.

HOW MUCH DATA SHARING?

From the point of view of cost, BPR promises to resolve a problem which has perplexed IT staff for several decades. Just how much data integration or sharing does a corporation need? A decade ago it was assumed that total integration was a worthwhile goal. As this proved unfeasible and unmanageable, firms fell back on systems which could be delivered quickly. While this produced benefits which were visible, they were not major.

The costs of systems development, staff retraining and implementation are known. Today we can associate a given level of data sharing with improvements in cycle time, cost and quality. This means we can introduce a quantifiable benefit into calculations for return on investment.

THE CHALLENGE OF BPR—TRANSITION

In addition to justifying cost, another issue presents itself. No corporation considering BPR today is a green field where systems are concerned. Indeed, because of the historical tendency to seek departmental solutions the existing systems may be implemented on a variety of hardware and software platforms. Many of the systems which exist are "mission critical" and cannot be thrown away or replaced overnight. The transition from the current situation to the future desired state is the major challenge for systems development and hence for BPR. Redesigning business processes may be the easy part!

While it is essential to have some statement of the ideal state (a target scenario), we must resign ourselves to the idea that this state may never be reached, and indeed that our vision of the ideal state may often be revised over the considerable period it will take to implement. In addition to this, even if the dream were realisable, the time scales would inevitably be too long to achieve the benefits required in a timely fashion. In the meantime we need a solution for today. The systems inventory at any point in time will inevitably consist of a mixture of old, new and enhanced systems. Key information flows may have been eliminated while others remain in place. The challenge of BPR is to find an IT transition strategy that recognises this reality and aims to get the business benefits some way.

In some instances replacement systems will be developed in parallel with existing systems and a "big bang" transition undertaken (with its inherent risks). More often, however, an evolutionary approach will be taken. It will be important to get the most out of existing systems. Where existing systems require enhancement it will often be possible to restructure or "reverse engineer" them to facilitate the changes. Sometimes packages or templates will fill a gap. New development will be appropriate where important new functionality is required. These components will be required to co-exist in heterogeneous hardware and software environments. Current trends in the industry are beginning to address this issue.

A recent leader of a BPR implementation project compared IT transition to surgery on a living body. We cannot do a total systems replacement overnight; our solutions must be commissioned one by one while not just maintaining but improving business performance.

BPR EXPLOITS NEW TECHNOLOGIES

Open systems provide the means to port systems from one environment to another with relative ease. In certain instances this will give the ability to consolidate databases previously on incompatible hardware platforms thereby eliminating information flows. Previously such database integration required redesign and rewriting of existing applications to run on the new common platform. I-CASE technology is beginning to support openness by automatically generating systems for a wide variety of hardware and software targets from a single application specification. In a recent case in Belgium three utility companies were merged. A power station system (running on IBM MVS/DB2 and generated by the IEF I-CASE tool) was required by another company with only Digital equipment. The application was regenerated by the IEF for VMS/RDB and tested in just two weeks.

Without integration with other departmental databases which are used within a process chain, information flows between departments are still physical, for example, pieces of paper. Islands of automation exist and the quality and speed of information remain a serious business issue (see Figure 5).

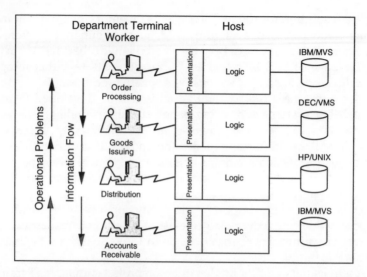

Figure 5 Islands of automation; quality and speed of information flows remain a serious business issue

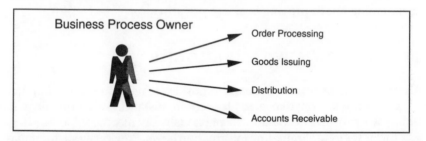

Figure 6 BPR empowers the "Business Process Owner" by providing access to information about the entire process chain

Often in BPR, a key issue is to identify a "business process owner" who will be responsible for the design and management of the entire process. This process worker must have adequate IT support to access information about the entire process chain (see Figure 6). By providing concurrent access to a variety of applications running on multiple hardware and software environments, the process owner is able to acquire process data, carry out one-stop business and continuously assess performance.

The key to enabling changes like these, and to the empowerment of process owners, is Client/Server technology. Client/Server applications give the opportunity to separate the "business end" (client) of an application from the complex data sharing end (server) which is perhaps on

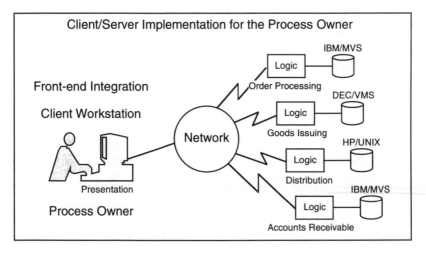

Figure 7 Front-end integration based on Client/Server, in a heterogeneous environment

a mainframe, as shown in Figure 7. It integrates other databases on different hardware and software platforms, enabling them to be accessed from the same application: this is called "desktop" or "front-end" integration. Front-end integration therefore provides access to information about the entire business process chain, even though this information is held on heterogeneous departmental servers.

In addition to empowering the process owner, BPR often examines the opportunity to integrate units of work around a set of so-called "case workers". Instead of one customer requirement being passed from specialist to specialist, as in a traditional manufacturing production line, IT can enable one person to carry out the entire range of tasks. The manufacturing equivalent is the handful of control engineering in an oil refinery which is highly automated.

Case workers are enabled by high levels of automation, such as integrated PC and corporate information systems, as well as by access to experts for assistance with exceptional situations.

An example is IBM Credit. IBM provides finance to its customers by means of its credit service. At one stage it took around 6 days to process one credit application. When IBM managers "walked through" the process they identified that on average the entire process actually took about 90 minutes and that the rest of the time the customer applications for credit were waiting in the in-trays or out-trays of specialist workers within the process chain. Furthermore, it was found, for example, that though a legal expert examined every credit application, in 80% of cases a standard contract applied.

The entire process was reorganised around a set of case workers each handling a single application from start to finish, calling on legal, financial and other experts to handle exceptional cases. While the precise IT solution selected by the BPR project is unknown, the project is a prime candidate for front-end integration, not just for the process owner as manager but also for the case workers as "doers".

With front-end integration, building one relatively simple front-end needs only a small project. The client process can itself be further improved as part of a continuous process improvement cycle.

Typically, the client end of the application runs on a workstation where it can be more easily tailored to customer requirements and more easily linked to other host, server and local PC applications and databases. Customer service is improved immediately along with process performance. Such front-end integration is exactly equivalent to the path adopted by the world's telecommunication companies to provide the service of International Subscriber Direct Dialling without replacing the colossal capital investment in existing installed equipment. This is undeniably invaluable to customers and to Telecomms suppliers' profitability. Like Client/Server, it solves the customer problem without any massive disruption to the underlying technology. Client/Server also enables the separation of the user requirements from the technical requirements.

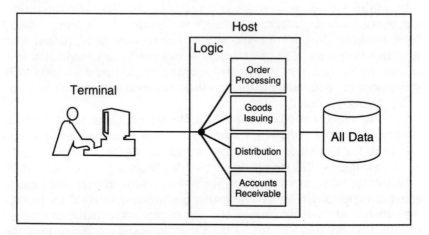

Figure 8 Back-end integration: an excellent solution, but more suited to an IT project rather than a BPR project

Another approach may be the host implementation of the BPR solution. This is called back-end integration, where applications are rebuilt and totally replaced, as shown in Figure 8. The end result may be an efficient, shareable database, but for BPR projects the time frames would be too lengthy, involving greater effort, costs and risks than a front-end approach. Server applications may be amended after a front-end project, if required. Back-end integration is therefore most suited to IT projects, as part of the housekeeping effort.

As technology begins to address the requirements of BPR the question naturally arises as to how this discipline fits with various systems development methodologies.

THE RELATIONSHIP BETWEEN BPR AND INFORMATION ENGINEERING

The use of existing heterogeneous hardware by open systems, downsizing, and Client/Server—all of these approaches to developing information systems are currently being subjected to the financial discipline of improved return on investment. As successes with BPR become visible, the question returns of how and where the IT development methodologies such as Information Engineering (IE) overlap with BPR.

Despite the fact that IE often succeeds in re-engineering business processes, and BPR often succeeds in defining information technology solutions, the two are substantially different. The objective of IE is to build high quality information systems fast and in line with business goals; the objective of BPR is to radically improve the performance of business processes even if in doing so the business goals have to be challenged and perhaps even changed. It is therefore as well to understand which objectives are being pursued so that on the one hand systems development is not paralysed by debate on the nature of the business, and on the other hand business decisions do not become subordinate to the needs of information technology.

IE attaches much importance to technology-independent models which express what the business does rather than how it does it. This is so because what is done changes much more slowly than how it is done. Systems based on these models therefore become working models of the business and in consequence are more robust, attracting significantly less maintenance activity. This strategy has been highly successful in producing systems which require little change once delivered.

BPR challenges what the business does as well as how it does it, in an attempt to identify radical change. Models which represent a relatively static situation are therefore of less interest. So too are technology-independent models, since technology may be a key determinant of how a process may be improved. Consequently, where IE is fairly prescriptive about which levels of detail and abstraction are appropriate to each stage of the method, BPR is happy to work simultaneously at multiple levels of abstraction and detail.

IE makes a virtue of dividing large problems into smaller ones. It does this by grouping those activities which are closely associated by their common use of data. This is an effective way of defining the building blocks which make up a system. These building blocks do, however, correspond in large measure to idealised functional boundaries and there is an assumption in analysis that either Information Strategy Planning or some other mechanism such as BPR will have already defined the larger picture; the approach works well as long as this assumption is validated.

BPR on the other hand starts by adopting a scope which is typically cross-functional in order to optimise the process holistically.

The perspective of IE is based on close coupling through data usage, while the perspective of BPR is on a cross-functional business process chain (see Figure 9). Having redesigned the business process there will inevitably be systems components to the solution. Equally inevitable is the ability to share data across the various functional units, one of the reasons for the resulting benefit. The broad scope of BPR therefore demands systems to support processes across functional boundaries which will be fairly broad in their scope and correspondingly difficult to manage. The building block

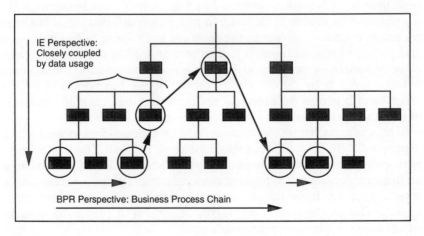

Figure 9   The different perspectives of BPR and IE

approach of IE is an effective method for managing detail across the scope.

BPR and IE use similar business modelling techniques, but while IE identifies the necessary detail to build application systems with common data, BPR identifies the business parameters required to improve process performance. As an example, if the procurement process is to be improved it will help if purchasing, goods receiving and accounts will see a common image of data about suppliers, products, purchase orders, deliveries, and invoices. In so far as this data co-exists in the same database, flows of information between the different functional units can be eliminated.

This will have beneficial effects on cycle times since access to the data will be instant and will also raise the possibility of organisational change taking place without disruption in the future. These benefits are the consequence of the enterprise-wide view of data encouraged by IE and its insistence on working independently of organisational structures. Nevertheless, data integration, which has a cost, takes place without adequate attention to the return on investment arising from the resulting process optimisation. BPR promises to provide this.

BPR brings into play consideration of key business metrics reflecting cycle time, cost and quality. It uses techniques such as Activity Based Costing, Process Simulation, and Quality Function Deployment. Activity Based Costing allocates costs to specific business processes; Process Simulation enables BPR practitioners to examine the impact of changing variables across the process chain; and Quality Function Deployment defines the quality parameters of a product and assigns the responsibility for achieving the desired quality levels back to the specific process in the process chain.

IE, on the other hand, is focused on information, and the way it is shared and processed. Therefore, BPR and IE are complementary, sharing an interest in business processes and data.

A typical BPR project may be divided into four phases: Initiation, Process Understanding, New Process Design and finally Implementation. During this time, the project team will engage in three BPR-specific activities: Information Gathering (informal), Process Modelling (formal), and Process Simulation (dynamic). They will identify the enterprise vision for the area under consideration, build a model of the "As Is" situation and then creatively develop potential "Should Be" scenarios for the future. Each scenario can be tested by simulation to enable the best solution to be chosen. The final phase, Implementation, involves primarily the people-oriented skills of the management of change.

IE starts from what the business is but does not try to change the business. BPR on the other hand is looking for radical performance increments and therefore seeks to change the business. If BPR is successful radical change is implied and this will cause upheaval within the business. This will not be welcomed on a routine basis. It is assumed therefore that the same process will not be revisited frequently. This means that IE's assumption of a relatively stable underlying reality will be justified. Incremental improvement will take over from BPR and will be the most common activity. A combination of relational database and I-CASE technologies has proved more than capable of dealing with such improvement with unprecedented speed and accuracy.

Clearly, all the BPR tasks involve the capture, reconciliation and manipulation of significant volumes of business information in a business model. To facilitate the management of this data, BPR requires software support to record these models, attach metrics to their components and analyse the results. Equally clearly, experience has shown the necessity of automation support through an integrated BPR tool to enable the necessary level of speed, quality and consistency with minimum risk in the chosen solution.

Both BPR and IE rely on business models. I-CASE tools also support the use of business models so ideally BPR tools and I-CASE tools should be able to share models. Based upon many years of internal experience, and supported by a programme of needs identification with major consulting houses, TI developed the Business Design Facility (BDF), a software tool running under Windows or OS/2 which actively supports the BPR practitioner. Moreover, since BPR and IE both work with the business objects of data and process, the BDF has an open interface enabling transfer in either direction with I-CASE tools other than the IEF (transfer is seamless with the IEF).

I-CASE tools should be able to generate systems directly from suitably enhanced business models. Because of this, systems today are being generated with unprecedented speed and accuracy. Despite this, it is still unfeasible to regenerate everything in sight. Packaged applications present one alternative, especially those generated by I-CASE tools and those which can be easily changed. There will ultimately be some components that can be supplied in a timely fashion only by changing existing systems.

To do this it is necessary, given the legacy of history, to restructure these systems into a form which is more readily comprehensible. Despite the fact that the holy grail of totally automatic software re-engineering is a dream, tools are emerging which can substantially assist restructuring by hand.

In terms of the flexibility of the BPR and IE, neither methodology is prescriptive in its approach. In the early 1980s, prescriptive methodologies were the vogue. The original version of the IE methodology and the IEF tool (the authors participated in their development) was highly prescriptive in determining the sequence in which phases and tasks were to be carried out. Experience has since shown that this approach is technically unnecessary and is not required by a significant proportion of the market.

In response, TI has evolved a flexible, highly customisable IE methodology and IEF tool which provides a stable framework encompassing all the activities performed in systems development. From within the framework, a variety of different development paths—alternative life cycles—can be chosen to suit the specific needs of the business. A range of practices, tasks, techniques and tools can be matched to the adopted development paths. The IE methodology today provides clear direction, and encourages parallel activities, consolidation and recycling using prototyping (simulation) to achieve the final desired solution.

In building the BPR methodology, TI's experience in constructing methodologies has been vital. Like the IE methodology, the BPR methodology provides clear direction, parallel activities, consolidation and recycling. The BDF has been designed as an open tool usable with a wide range of BPR methodologies. Accordingly TI's BPR methodology is available, but is optional for the BDF. We expect many of our customers to have already selected or at least identified a particular method, either with us or maybe with one of the many third-party BPR consulting houses.

THE BUSINESS DESIGN FACILITY

The BDF is a software tool supporting every member of the project team. The BDF allows businesses to be modelled and specific processes highlighted for purposes of analysis (see Figures 10 and 11). It links to other tools and has a seamless interface to the IEF which is now the world's leading I-CASE tool in terms of both installed inventory and customer satisfaction expressed through surveys.

There is a growing pool of IEF generated applications (templates) which are available to users of IEF. Some are developed by TI but many others by users. In the first category are financial systems (General Ledger, Accounts Payable etc.) and the investment management system MAXIMIS. In the latter are a Frequent Flyer Bonus system, a procurement system and an order management system.

In the area of software re-engineering TI is collaborating with Price Waterhouse whose ARRAE tool is the most powerful software available in this area to date.

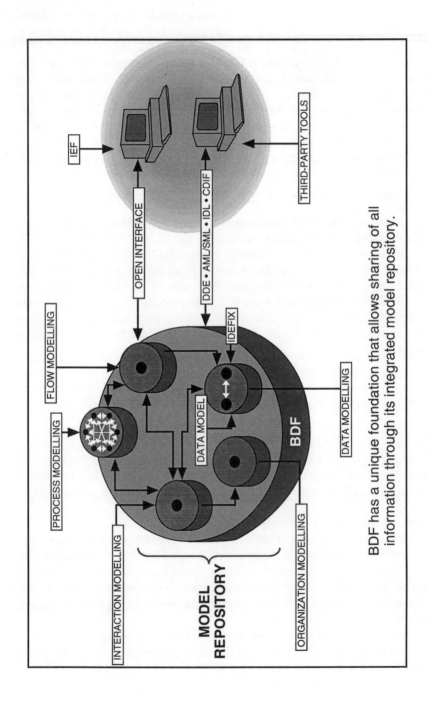

BDF has a unique foundation that allows sharing of all information through its integrated model repository.

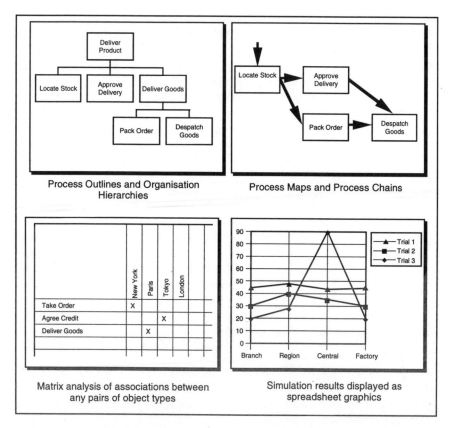

Figure 11 Examples of some of the standard BPR analytic diagrams supported by the BDF

SUMMARY

We would not like to leave readers with false hopes or concepts. No tool will ever re-engineer a business. BPR analysis and the implementation of solutions is very much human-based, involving objectives setting, identifying constraints, managing change, and many other activities. However, there is much that computer automation can do, as summarised in Figure 12.

Clearly then, the enterprising organisation today can exploit a range of effective BPR methodologies and can support them with an emerging range of powerful software tools. Experience and business information

Computer Support for Business	Purpose	Technology Needed	TI's Tool
Understand	Reengineer and optimise business processes.	Data Collection Process Modelling Process Simulation	BDF. Feeds process definitions into the IEF for BPR Implementation.
Develop	Develop integrated information systems.	I-CASE tool for systems development life cycle.	IEF. Feeds its process definitions into the BDF.
Operate	Enable more effective business services and products.	For example: Hosts systems Client/Server Workstations	IEF for Client/Server
Automate	Minimum supervision of fully automated processes.	Data Collection Real-Time control Monitors Alarms	REAL TIME TOOLS

Figure 12 Automated support for BPR

gathered in existing I-CASE tools can be used where desired as a starting point for the BPR project and results can be fed into such I-CASE tools to enable the design and generation of revised systems to support the redesigned business processes.

Open systems with the ability to harness the existing investment in systems on heterogeneous platforms can be supported by improved I-CASE tools which enable powerful Client/Server application systems to be built on top of or by replacement of existing systems.

As Dr Hammer has stated, now is the time to stop paving the cow paths.

11

Technology and Business Process Re-Engineering: Identifying Opportunities for Competitive Advantage

Linda Hickman

ABSTRACT

A new approach to business and information systems development is emerging with Business Process Re-Engineering (BPR). Increasing numbers of business managers are looking at BPR as a means to apply information technology to their business in order to gain competitive advantage and provide quality products and services to their customers.

BPR is based on a recognition that many business processes span the entire organisation, whereas, typically, systems development has been concentrated on functional areas within an organisation. Unfortunately, a functional approach can lead to a fragmentation in processing information and creates breaks in the business processing. With BPR, the design of efficient and effective business processes is the first step towards building

Software Assistance for Business Re-engineering. Edited by Kathy Spurr, Paul Layzell, Leslie Jennison and Neil Richards a business system, before usage of information technology to improve a business process.

The world of information systems development is characterised by detail and much of the detail is centred around aspects of the technology: functionality, hardware and network configuration details. It is not surprising, then, if the business side is neglected. The main point of using technology to improve the competitive position of the business is usually lost by the emphasis on the technical development issues—on the *how*, rather than the *why*.

Systems developers are seeking tools and techniques to assist in the analysis required for business complexity. Understanding the dynamic complexity of organisations goes beyond traditional systems analysis techniques and the methods which usually sought completeness through detail. Indeed, too often a binary view of the world seemed inherent in systems development—business complexity was ignored and oversimplified when it would not fit into the narrow confines of the technical solution. In this paper, we explore the integrative approach of value-chain analysis used by business analysts.

BPR offers a tremendous challenge to systems developers. It will require a new approach to systems development, one which is based on proactively contributing to improvements in business processes. Using case examples drawn from current business practitioners and the international consulting experience of the author, the paper will show how the techniques of business process engineering can be used to approach systems development from a stronger business perspective.

INTRODUCTION

A new view on the potential business use of Information Technology is emerging with Business Process Re-Engineering. Today, the application of technology to business operations has often fallen short of the expectations of business managers. What has been the basis for the shortfall? Basically, business management often cannot obtain integrated information about their business from the type of information systems they are using. They know that it might be possible, but have given the task to technical specialists who often narrowly apply technology. A broader understanding of the business and the potential leverage of information technology is needed by information systems developers.

An approach which attempts to draw business and the application of information technology closer together is Business Process Re-Engineering (BPR). BPR is based on a recognition that many business processes span the entire organisation (enterprise), whereas, typically, systems development has been concentrated on functional areas within an organisation. A functional approach can lead to a fragmentation in processing information and create breaks in the business processing. With BPR, the design of efficient and effective business processes is the first step towards building a business system, then selection of information technology to improve a business process.

Traditionally, organisations were divided into specialised functional areas such as sales, marketing, and engineering, as a part of a management approach to break down tasks and have specialists in each. Unfortunately, vertical division by functions often leads to barriers in procedures and information flow across the organisation. We have all observed the results which have data and information duplicated in many places without sufficient coordination. But it is not just a redundancy of data that we are concerned about (although that is the symptom that systems developers often observe); there is a more fundamental flaw in organising around functions—the whole view of a business process is often fragmented beyond recognition by any one manager. Lacking a holistic view, business decisions and the business processes become vulnerable, especially in a dynamic environment where complex interrelationships determine the very survival of a business.

In the world outside the organisation, there have also been traditional divisions which create boundaries (barriers).The boundaries of organisations formerly were defined by roles such as customers, competitors, suppliers, government regulatory agencies and so forth. Just as the internal view of the organisation is fragmented by vertical divisions, an external view loses coherence and flexibility when boundaries are created between organisations.

There is a growing recognition that traditional structures and the flow of information within and between them no longer work well in 1993. There is a need to create a view which one executive of General Electric called a 'boundaryless' company: one which does not have barriers between traditional functions, 'domestic' and 'foreign' operations and groups within the organisation. Technological advances in information systems, such as relational technology, create the potential for integrated systems, but even that has not been implemented to its full competitive business advantage. Too often underlying business processes are not re-examined during the course of information systems development. The new approach requires an open inquiry into *what the business is trying to achieve*, the means by which it is working to those ends and the results of the business activities and processes. Such a fundamental investigation must necessarily be driven by business management and include the entire enterprise and industry context. The examination should move freely across traditional, functional and organisational boundaries.

DEVELOPING A BUSINESS PERSPECTIVE

The world of systems developers is characterised by detail and much of the detail is centred around aspects of the technology: software functionality, hardware and network configuration details. It is not surprising then to find that the business side of systems development is the neglected side. Unfortunately, this neglect has a long-term devastating effect on the use of information technology. There are too many systems that are only technically functioning, that is, they hold data, run programs, generate reports. But, the systems are not helping the business to grow and be competitive. In fact some systems can hinder business change. One writer reports on a company which restructured its business by throwing out computer systems which actually created delays in the complete business process.

What goes wrong in a system like that? Certainly, everyone had different intentions. The problem is one of perspective and translating that perspective into clear requirements that will guide the use of information technology to support the business. The perspective is usually too narrow. For example, looking at an accounting system in isolation from customer and supplier transactions, or a perspective which leads to automating a manual process without considering if that process has efficient steps or if the steps are even necessary with new technology or whether the business currently needs that same process.

In a Harvard Business Review article which provided the impetus for much of the discussion on BPR, Michael Hammer wrote of a dramatic change in the handling of accounts payable at Ford (Hammer, 1990). The change in the business process was only feasible with the new technology now available. Traditionally, a purchase order was sent to a supplier, the supplier sent the goods with a document which accompanied delivery. At a later point the supplier sent an invoice for those goods which had been delivered and Ford checked the invoice against the delivery documentation. When everyone was satisfied that the goods on invoice were the goods on the purchase order and the goods which were accepted and delivered, a request for payment could be issued which would lead to payment of the supplier. The process could be lengthy and it required a large number of persons to complete the steps.

When Ford looked at a competitor, Mazda, a very different process was discovered. This provided Ford with a 'benchmark' for time and resources.

They found that less than a dozen persons handled the process which took hundreds at Ford; the difference was the application of technology. Using EDI and bar code readers, the process changed fundamentally. No paperwork was required; a bar code reading of the goods received both triggered the recording of the acceptance of the goods as well as triggered raising payment to the supplier. In the new process the traditional purchase orders, invoices and requests for payment were substituted with transaction information which handled the full process with the supplier from order to payment. In business terms, the process was 're-engineered' with time and cost savings.

The Ford case is a good one to examine. How do we identify processes within any organisation which can be improved and re-engineered? To help answer that question, we need to take a brief look at business trends in the 1990s and the years beyond to begin to understand the business context.

Business Trends

Major structural changes are occurring within organisations and between organisations. These are attempts to respond to complex, dynamic, global changes. While it is beyond the scope of the paper to discuss all the causes, some of the key business trends are presented in outline to understand the current business perspective.

The major trends in structures which have been well documented include:

- organisational restructuring
- globalisation
- rapid technological advances
- movement towards a knowledge/information society

If we take each of the trends, we can see a common underlying thread: rapid interchange of information, made feasible by telecommunication developments and other technological advances. The emphasis on organisational restructuring is manifest in several ways. Organisations will be moving toward smaller units which may be combined into federal groups. Charles Handy, a leading British expert in management, suggests that the possibility of creating a federal structure is due to the opportunities afforded by information technology. IT enables a structure which can have integrated, smaller units based around a moderate-sized centre (Handy, 1992). Another aspect of organisational restructuring will be to change

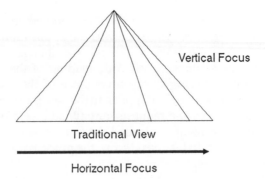

Figure 1   Organisation view

the shape from a tall pyramid with many layers to a flatter organisation with a horizontal emphasis or perhaps even a circle such as the structure introduced at BAXI in the UK. These structures are quite distinct from the familiar vertical slices.

The implication for systems is clear—a process across the organisation will be conducted differently than a functionally organised process. Recall the Ford example: many functional areas were traditionally involved, and in systems terms, often the data held by different functional areas was held in different forms. The patchwork quilt of systems was changed to a seamless process.

A Japanese management expert, Kenichi Ohmae, has made an observation regarding the globalisation of organisations. He tells us that the flow of information across geographic borders is helping to reshape the global map, regardless of political boundaries (Ohmae, 1991). The global enterprise is created and sustained through new technology.

Again, in the second trend towards globalisation, we find the central importance of information systems. How will we approach developing systems for organisations which will facilitate cross-border transactions and the flow of information? We can't support that type of business activity with a 'stand-alone system' mentality.

The development of sophisticated telecommunication networks will be a related tool for globalisation. These are the foundations for international information highway systems. Just as the traditional infrastructure for delivering goods and conducting commerce was based on highways on land, air, and sea, a new type of highway is now emerging—Tom Peters refers to them as 'electronic highway systems' (Peters, 1992). In developing economies, including those emerging in Eastern Europe, it is now often easier to conduct business internationally through satellite communications than within the borders of the countries which still have underdeveloped systems. Developers of systems can leap-frog development stages and have the opportunity to learn from the failures of isolated systems.

The trend of rapid technological advances speaks for itself. We are well aware of the acceleration of all aspects of developing and producing in a world where product life cycles are continually shortening. How do we support organisations which produce and deliver services in such an environment? The systems and processes will have to be built around understanding what the organisation is trying to achieve—at a very, very basic or generic (core) level. Flexibility is inherent to survival in such a dynamic world. For systems development, that will require a business understanding which is at a higher level than the details of a CURRENT business activity.

The most fundamental structural change is all-encompassing as we see the trend to move from an industrial, production-based society to one which is an Information Society. The strength of the trend has been reported by many economists and writers. One prediction is that 80 percent of economic value will stem from information technology by 2020 (Peters, 1992).

With the background of such a changing business perspective in mind, we will now focus the next section on an overview of the BPR approach which is emerging as a response to the challenge to implement major restructuring. Every organisation will face the need to re-engineer if it is to survive in a world which is in transition.

The Business Process Re-Engineering (BPR) Approach

At a recent forum on BPR with representatives from European organisations, one of the major themes surrounded the question of 'what is BPR?'—many organisations are in the process of changes which come under labels which either are BPR or are later claimed to be BPR. The Chief Executive of BAXI said that for their company it was bringing together a number of initiatives, such as JIT, quality circles, etc. into one company-wide programme for restructuring the organisation. While there are a number of techniques for re-engineering a business, there is not one commonly agreed set of principles; thus it is most appropriately labelled an approach, not a method for change.

There are some common characteristics to the approach which most practitioners will include in their conduct of re-engineering.

The basics of BPR include:

1. a process orientation
2. a horizontal focus across boundaries (rather than a vertical, functional approach within an organisation)
3. a customer perspective
4. benchmarking performance measures
5. building organisational capabilities/competencies
6. empowerment of individuals in the organisation
7. improvement through application of information technology

A business process view is the central theme in BPR. While there may be differing definitions in use, we have found it useful in our consultancy to think of a business process as one which is a logical series of dependent activities which use the resources of the organisation to create or result in an observable or measurable outcome, such as a product or service.

A business process usually crosses functional and organisational boundaries, thus there is a stronger horizontal focus. Looking at the Ford example, the business process was *'obtaining and paying for supplies'*. That was an integrated view which cut across the traditional purchasing, receiving and accounts payable functions. In most organisations, those three activities are in separate functional departments.

In the initial stage of BPR, an organisation identifies critical processes to the business which are important to the customer and clients. Measures of performance are developed which can be benchmarks for comparison of the performance of a similar process used or designed by others. In this way, methods for improving current practices are identified.

Another guiding principle in BPR is to examine the business process from a customer perspective. One hospital which has undergone a complete restructuring placed the patients at the top of their structural chart and then developed the concept of patient-care teams. When the patient became the primary focus, there were fundamental organisational changes which broke down the barriers between specialisations within the hospital. The changes permitted a more efficient and effective flow in the process of treating the patient.

The fourth feature, benchmarking performance, is at the heart of the techniques which are used in BPR. Performance measures, such as manufacturing cycle time, delivery time, inventory size, quality, are observed for the organisation and then benchmarked against other organisations—the leaders in an industry. Often the gaps are so great, it leads to focusing on improvements in an area, usually with the result of re-engineering a process to be more similar to the one with better benchmark results. It is always revealing how great the gaps can be for the same process within different organisations.

In a 'Lean Enterprise Benchmarking Project' undertaken in the automotive components sector in Japan and the UK, there were very many differences observed. Just one of the examples will give a flavour of the magnitude. In the world-class plants, inventory was a mere one-seventh of the other plants. Their stock turnover ratio was also three times higher in contrast to prevailing practices (Arthur Anderson & Co., 1993). The quantitative benchmarks provide a basis for re-examination and then re-engineering processes.

Strengths as well as weaknesses are the basis for BPR benchmarking. The assessment of capabilities and competencies which are critical in the industry is another business analysis technique. A core (basic) capability is a business strength that drives the business. If we take the case of a manufacturing company, we might determine that business development requires core capabilities in the areas of new product development, new customer development, design and engineering skills, manufacturing, supply chain management, customer services and global ventures.

Building core capabilities is tied not only to performance benchmarking, but also fundamentally to developing a different view of the roles of individuals in an organisation. When we look at organisations which have been successful in implementing BPR, we find that restructuring was always accompanied by empowerment. With empowerment, individuals have the responsibility for wider participation in decision making and for taking immediate actions. At Mutual Benefit Life, their redesigned business process allows just one person to make all the decisions regarding an insurance application that were formerly made by several staff. In other organisations it can be giving each individual a responsible role on a cross-functional team. The degree of empowerment is often visibly measurable by the number of layers of management which have decreased.

The seventh and last of the BPR components on our list is the improvement of business processes through the application of information technology. The enabling technology for the Ford case included EDI and bar code readers, and for Mutual Benefit Life, an expert system of rules to assist in handling cases. Creative application of information technology is an important aspect of BPR. In the second section of this paper, other cases of enabling technology will be described.

These seven key features of BPR are handled in different ways by various organisations. The techniques used for BPR combine techniques from information systems development methods, such as CASE Method, and business analysis techniques, such as value-chain analysis. It is the tighter integration of business analysis with information technology which is especially important in this approach. While a top-down approach as advocated by CASE Method provides a basis for documenting important strategic business needs, the integration with business decision making which is required to implement business changes is generally considered outside the scope of the information systems development life cycle.

Systems developers who are responsible for strategic enterprise models often find areas in the business which could benefit from change. The very activity of developing an enterprise model creates an opportunity for observing business processes across the organisation. Frequently, redundant or inefficient flows or information are traced. The dilemma is how to effectively approach a business change from within a task which had been established for developing an information system. Despite very astute observations that may come from an information systems strategy study, the means to implement business change are usually not within the original scope.

The crucial difference with using a BPR approach is the acknowledgment that *both* business and information technology specialists must work together in order to achieve significant business competitive advantage. We will identify some creative applications of technology in the next section.

INFORMATION TECHNOLOGY FOR COMPETITIVE ADVANTAGE

One of the basic management tasks for a retailer is to ensure that the right amount of stock of goods is available. If there is too much, it is costing money to hold it; if there is not enough, sales are lost. Many retail businesses eventually fail because they do not get the balance right, often enough. Or, if they do not fail, they still see their customers going to a competitor who may have the item in stock. When the retail business is based on the premise of 24 hour service, running out of stock is especially a serious problem. In order to eliminate the feast/famine cycle of stock which can occur and to provide high level customer service, the 7-Eleven chain of 24 hour food/beverage outlets applied a combination of information technology possibilities. A Point-of-Sale (POS) tracking system is linked to a stock delivery system which is integrated to a supplier system.

The total system thus uses the point-of-sales terminals to track sales, then to calculate stock replenishment, allocate deliveries three times a day and calculate payments and receipts for deliveries/suppliers. That is business processing re-engineering, if we compare it to what the previous situation would have been—one that we all know from experience in observing retail operations. Consider all the possibilities for POS terminals alone!

The 7-Eleven example shows the connection between retailer and distributor. Another example goes one step further back in the industry chain. A US retailer, Dillard's is a clothing store. When the inventory of stock falls below a certain level, the apparel manufacturer, Haggar, is notified electronically. If Haggar does not have the cloth in stock to manufacture the order, the textile manufacturer, Burlington Industries, is also notified electronically. The electronic data interchange (EDI) thus creates strong links in the industry chain thus reducing delays and cutting costs substantially.

In each of the examples, the enabling technology ensures that the most important information for the process is communicated to the most appropriate point as rapidly as possible. Asking the basic business question: *'what is it you are trying to achieve?'* and looking at what information is needed to achieve that business purpose is the beginning of re-engineering most processes. At 7-Eleven, 24 hour service means that all items should be on the shelf at all times for customers. In order to achieve that business purpose, complete information about stock must be rapidly known to everyone in the process at all times as soon as one single item moves.

BUSINESS ANALYSIS AND REQUIREMENTS SPECIFICATION FOR BPR

The questions posed earlier—how do you identify processes in an organisation which can be improved by re-engineering? how do you identify opportunities for applying information technology?—require analytical techniques and tools for answers.

Identifying techniques for designing systems which fulfil business purpose, provide competitive advantage and are part of a re-engineering effort is a challenge. It requires the ability to envisage the organisation in a holistic and dynamic manner. It is like listening to a symphony and hearing each individual note played—knowing the full score as the conductor must.

Many of the methods for systems analysis have concentrated on obtaining detail of the organisation's information needs. Often the detail obscures the possibility of obtaining a broad view of the entire organisation. There is another issue. The models, such as an Entity-Relationship model or Data Flow diagrams, have limitations. They usually concentrate on showing detail complexity; however, that is not the complete picture. In fact, it is the assumption that we have a complete picture if we include all the details which is especially misleading.

Peter Senge points out that there is both complexity of detail as well as dynamic complexity (Senge, 1990). Dynamic complexity is the more diffuse type. Often, activity is not in a simple cause and effect chain (for which we can find detail), but rather dynamic interrelationship between parts of a system cause different (often unexpected) effects at different times. Dynamic complexity has not been a part of our systems modelling.

In addition to traditional systems modelling techniques such as Entity-Relationship models, function and process models, and other techniques which are primarily focused on representing information usage for computerisation, BPR introduces the use of business analysis tools.

There are various organisational analysis techniques which can be usefully applied to our attempt to obtain a broad business perspective and an understanding of dynamic interrelationships. Porter's Value-Chain analysis is one useful tool to help view processes within an organisation and across an industry/sector. It is presented briefly in outline form to provide an example of its potential.

Using Value Chain Analysis

Value Chain analysis provides a paradigm or framework for an analyst to document the use of information across an organisation. The basic premise was outlined by Porter in 1985. It has been in use by business analysts, but often neglected by systems analysts.

The value chain includes those activities which add value for which customers are willing to pay for a product or service. The customer provides the end focal point. Therefore, activities which do not add value to a product or service from the customer perspective are areas to explore for potential change or omission. As Figure 2 illustrates, there are nine value activities categorised as either primary or support activities.

Each activity has both a physical and an information component. In the past, application of technology has usually focused on the physical component of the activity, for example, robotics in manufacturing. Now systems analysts can approach the value chain as a means of identifying areas which can apply information technology for greatest business benefit in the value chain.

The linkages between the value activities also contribute to overall understanding of the value chain. Tightly coupled activities can reduce time and costs, for example. In BPR, we can examine a business process across the value chain and evaluate the linkages between activities and to the other chains in the value system, e.g., supplier and customer. It is an aid to help identify opportunities to improve the business process. We are

SUPPORT ACTIVITIES

Administration & Infrastructure					Value Added – Cost = Profit
Human Resources					
Technology Development					
Resource Procurement					
Inbound Logistics	Operation	Outbound Logistics	Marketing & Sales	Service	

PRIMARY ACTIVITIES

Figure 2   Value chain (adapted from Porter 1985)

looking for points in the business process where changes can be made or need improvement, such as

1. unnecessary process steps (non-value added)
2. duplicated tasks and data
3. conflicting or contradictory steps with the process
4. blockages and time lags at linkage points
5. time-consuming, error-prone manual procedures
6. below-average benchmarks for time and cost of steps
7. other factors limiting efficiency or quality in the process

The guiding question is 'what are we trying to achieve?'. The 7-Eleven retail store example if examined from the value-chain perspective shows weaknesses such as potential blockages and time lags before the redesign.

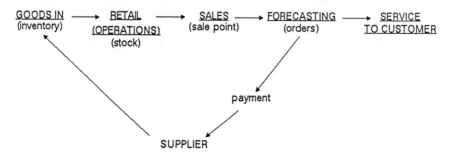

Figure 3   7-Eleven before redesign

If we look carefully at the diagram, we can identify potential delays at several linkage points and most critically between sales and orders. Next, when we examine the process with the business goal of providing 24 hour walk-in service to customers (while meeting the typical business objectives of low inventory costs, adequate stock-on-hand and fast response by suppliers to re-stock), it becomes apparent that any delays could jeopardise the goal and objectives. Therefore, the process cycle time needs to be shortened. The customer is paying for the value-added convenience of 24 hour availability—therefore any activities which could delay orders or are affected by a lack of real-time information on stock should become the focus area. The redesigned process shown in Figure 4 represents the POS terminals/ordering/payment system described earlier.

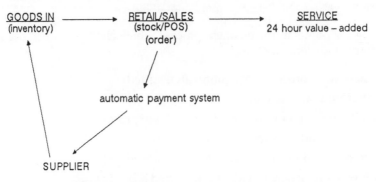

Figure 4   7-Eleven after redesign

With the introduction of the POS terminals linked to ordering and payment systems, several time lags have been eliminated and the number of deliveries have been increased, thus enabling achievement of the business goal for 24 hour service and the related business objectives.

The total process cycle has been decreased and the costs of inventory lowered. That creates a value-added service for the customer who will pay extra for immediate access to goods on a 24-hour daily basis. The redesigned process was made feasible through a creative application of information technology and a good understanding of the competitive requirements of the business.

Tool Support for BPR

BPR is a process itself. The process of redesigning is the subject of much current discussion regarding tool support. As noted earlier, BPR requires an integrated approach. That is especially true for tool support. There is no single tool or technique which will suffice for BPR. Such a view would be reductionist and lead to oversimplifications.

The goal will be to use an integrated toolset, often from various vendors, which can be integrated around a common repository. Much of the tool support for business system development which exists today was designed separately and has a limited capability for integration. A first and near term step is to improve the degree of integrations for KEY information that is to be shared and accessed by the tool set. Given the capability to integrate existing tools, we can then build on the existing investment and experience invested in CASE, applications and other software tools.

New tools for BPR must meet the requirement of integrations to fully capture dynamic business complexity.

CONCLUSION

BPR offers a tremendous challenge to systems developers. It will require a new approach to systems development, one which is based on proactively applying information technology to improve business processes. This can be accomplished by:

- adopting a business perspective
- improving business and organisational knowledge
- viewing processes across organisational boundaries
- proposing creative business solutions with information technology
- developing advanced, integrated CASE tools for BPR
- participating as a member of a cross-functional team

In a world which is making a transition to the Information Society, systems developers are well placed to play leading roles.

BIBLIOGRAPHY

1. Arthur Anderson & Co. 1993. The Lean Enterprise Benchmarking Project Report. London.
2. Drucker Peter F. 1993. *Post-Capitalist Society*. Butterworth-Heinemann Ltd, Oxford.
3. Feigenbaum E. McCorduck P. and Nii H.P. 1988. *The Rise of the Expert Company* Macmillan, London.

4. Hammer Michael. Reengineering Work: Don't Automate, Obliterate. *Harvard Business Review.* July-August 1990.
5. Handy Charles. 1992. Balancing Corporate Power: A New Federalist Paper *Harvard Business Review.* Vol 70. No 6.
6. Harrington H. James. 1991. *Business Process Improvement.* McGraw-Hill Inc, New York.
7. Hirschon L. and Gilmore T. The New Boundaries of the 'Boundaryless' company. *Harvard Business Review* (EI), Vol.70.No 3.
8. Ohmae Kenichi. 1991. *The Borderless World* Harper Collins, London.
9. Peters Tom. 1992. *Liberation Management.* Necessary Disorganisation for the Nanosecond Nineties. Macmillan, London.
10. Porter Michael E. 1985. *Competitive Advantage* Free Press, London.
11. Porter Michael E., and Millar Victor 1991. *How Information Gives You Competitive Advantage.* Harvard Business Review Paperback Series, Boston.
12. Senge P. 1990. *The Fifth Discipline: The Art and Practice of the Learning Organisation.* Doubleday, New York.
13. G. Stalk.Philip E. Shulman I. 1992. Competing on Capabilities: The New Rules of Corporate Strategy. *Harvard Business Review* Vol. 70. No 2.
14. Ward John. 1991. *Strategic Planning for Information Systems.* John Wiley & Sons, New York.

Questions and Answers from the Panel Session

1. Given the traditional approach to corporate organisation as depicted by the triangle below, where would you feel that Business Re-Engineering fits?

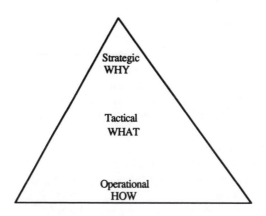

Some commentators feel that Business Re-Engineering applies at the lower operational levels. Others believe that it is necessary to address strategic issues and business goals before dealing with operational processes, which inevitably

Software Assistance for Business Re-engineering. Edited by Kathy Spurr, Paul Layzell,
Leslie Jennison and Neil Richards
© 1993 John Wiley & Sons Ltd

must be a mechanistic implementation leading towards the business goals. (Kathy Spurr)

Mills: A range of tools can be used for all levels of business activity (strategic through to operational). BPR is trying to do more than continuous process improvement. I agree with Michael Hammer's advice that we should look at the macro level and challenge the rules of the business, and so achieve big improvements.

Born: Apache addresses the lower operational levels very well, but through the models which it produces, it does help pinpoint strategic and tactical issues.

Huckvale: RADS (Role Activity Diagrams) can be used at all levels. We have used them successfully at senior management levels, capturing the 'big' picture, and at lower operational levels.

Dale: Re-engineering is strategic; simplification is tactical; process improvement is operational, using the terms defined in my own paper.

2. In addition, why does there seem to be so much emphasis on business processes? In contrast, in the area of software, many experts currently are moving away from the use of process models as a basis for the design of software, preferring instead to focus on the objects in the system, and the strategic system objectives. This generally leads to a much more robust, flexible and durable design, which matches the true requirements of the system. (Kathy Spurr)

Farhoodi: Object-oriented is a promising way forward. CADDIE uses an object-oriented approach, which can be applied at all levels of the business.

Born: Business Re-engineering can use an object-oriented approach to objects in the real world, and it must take humans and their interactions into account.

Huckvale: I agree with Gary. The formal modelling language SPML that complements RADs is indeed object-oriented.

{Editor's comment: Following the panel session, there was discussion on this question amongst some of the speakers. Whilst most speakers agreed that object-oriented techniques were beneficial, there was a sense that clients undergoing a business re-engineering exercise may think in terms of their business processes. This is because the business processes to a certain extent identify the business. Hence the term 'process' can be used for the benefit of the BRE clients. However, the business engineer may use whichever techniques are appropriate to analyse and re-engineer the business.}

3. Some presenters suggested that organisations should be radical in their thinking. Apart from Logica, which presenters have brought radical thinking to their processes? (Jim Farrow)

Huckvale: ICL has been using Business Re-engineering techniques for some time, and it has changed radically what it is doing as a business and its perception of what its customers want.

Dale: I have worked on business processes that cross many businesses around the globe. The re-engineering work involved changes to distribution logistics; new customer support centre organisations; an international computer network, as well as transfer of profits between businesses across international boundaries.

4. If it is not too early yet, what impact is the availability of tools having on Business Re-engineering methods and the range of problems that can be tackled? (Leslie Jennison)

Huckvale: Using tools helps business people to see the possibilities.

Hickman: There are two types of process to distinguish between. There is the process of conducting BRE. Then, there is another process involving changes to the business processes themselves. The process of conducting BRE can use tools and techniques, but tools do not change the business processes. Changing the business processes involves change management and organisatioal issues not addressed by our seminar.

Watts: Just as CASE tools automate aspects of the system delivery process, so process redesign tools can automate aspects of the process of designing processes. The main thing is to avoid making the mistakes that were (and are) made with the introduction of CASE tools—which automated individual activities within the existing systems delivery process. Organisations need to work out how they will go about redesigning business processes and then select an integrated set of tools which support the complete process of process redesign.

The ideal situation is where the approaches to business re-engineering and systems delivery are seamlessly integrated and supported by an integrated set of software tools.

5. Is organisational capability a barrier to effective process re-engineering? What can you do if it is? (Aidan Ward)

Born: Look at the SEI model of maturity in software engineering for guidance here, and don't expect to migrate any business process through more than one change of level of maturity at a time.

Watts: The value stream can be used to identify the skills required for each redesign option. The organisation's capability to implement the option can then be assessed—are the skills already available, can they be learned, can they be bought in?

Skills are one aspect of organisational capability. The key aspects to analyse are the cultural and political factors which make a redesign option unworkable. For example, it is essential to identify the informal coalitions involved in the current process and assess the impact of each of the redesign options on each coalition. It is relatively easy to come up with an excellent redesigned process, but harder to manage all the cultural and organisational aspects of the change. It is important for people carrying out business re-engineering to learn change management skills and techniques as well as process modelling skills.

Dale: Change can still be achieved if you are prepared to be radical. Do the top level design first, then check the management skills. In one case in my experience a policy decision was taken that if necessary all managers would be reselected according to the requirements of the new process roles.

Farhoodi: There are limits to how many variables an individual can juggle or evaluate when presented with the results of a situation.

6. One of the speakers said that tools and diagrams for modelling should be intuitively obvious—none of the ones I have seen so far could be described as such. Why is this? Is it because Business Re-engineering just isn't intuitively obvious? Or is it because everybody is taking a bottom-up analysis approach? (Carol Byde)

Mills: As an industry, we are still at the prototyping stage of BRE tool design. I expect the tool interfaces to change significantly as we gain more experience of their use.

Haynes: It is only possible to make tools intuitively obvious if users share a common paradigm. We should recognise that there is no common paradigm at present. These tools may be used by the IT department, the Quality department as well as departments within the organisation itself. There is no common paradigm in place for all these users at present.

Huckvale: It was I who made the comment about the need for tools to be intuitively obvious. I can only reiterate that we have found that users at all levels have no trouble in reading Role Activity Diagrams. This is probably because they emphasise what people actually do, rather than the data they do it to.

Stevenson: Users have had a favourable reaction to the presentation of results from the tool ɪthink.

Watts: You might like to refer to the sections in my paper about 'plan and position the BRE project' and the framework for integrating the various initiatives.

7. If a business process spans many business functions, how should we deal with traditional hierarchical organisation structures? That is, how can we get sponsorship for necessary Business Re-Engineering initiatives? How do quality initiatives affect Business Re-Engineering? (G Peacock)

Dale: Sponsorship has to be there. If it is not already there, you can't go and seek it. Business Re-Engineering has nothing to do with Quality as defined by BSI or ISO standards. It is closely allied to total quality management but requires a higher level of thinking.

Born: The real world which Business Re-Engineering addresses includes regulation and quality standards. Business Re-Engineering must take this into account by making quality part of the business.

8. Is BPR a solution in search of a problem? (J R Greer)

Mills: Not at all. The pressures on business are so great that people are desperately searching for answers. Yes, there is hype about Business Re-Engineering, but it does offer techniques for change. Only those businesses that can learn to adapt quickly can survive.

Section 4

Some Tools for Business Re-Engineering

Leslie Jennison

The last section of this book contains overviews of the tools described in these papers and demonstrated at the Business Process Re-Engineering Seminar. The intention is to provide enough information for you to decide if you are interested in evaluating or using any of these specific tools, together with UK and USA contact points so that you can obtain further details.

The editors would like to thank the authors of papers and demonstrators of tools for supplying the information, which is correct at the time of the Seminar in June 1993. Details appear in tool name sequence. For each tool there is a short description giving:

- The name of the originating organisation

- The status of the software: whether it is commercially available, for proprietary use only, or a research tool

- The year of introduction

- An indication of the price: in most cases this depends so much on options and the provision of other services, so suppliers were asked to assign the price per tool user to one of the following bands—lower (less than

Software Assistance for Business Re-engineering. Edited by Kathy Spurr, Paul Layzell,
Leslie Jennison and Neil Richards
© 1993 John Wiley & Sons Ltd

£500 or $500), medium (around £2000 or $2000) or upper (£5–8000 or $5–8000)—but some suppliers have chosen to provide prices on application

- The name and address of the supplier in the United Kingdom, and in the USA

- The Key Features as stated by the supplier

- The supplier's brief description of Methodology support

- Operating environments in which the software can be used for re-engineering projects; some suppliers have also specified the target environments in which any generated solution software may be run

- Interfaces to other tools

- A short illustration, provided by the supplier, of the structure or capability of the software

The inclusion of products in this book is for informational purposes only, and constitutes neither an endorsement nor a recommendation of quality or fitness for purpose. The publisher and editors assume no responsibility with regard to the performance or use of these products.

This is not intended to be a complete catalogue of tools that can be used for business re-engineering. The editors are happy to receive information about other tools for re-engineering.

APACHE

Originator:

EDS Corporation

Status:

Proprietary

Supplier in United Kingdom:

EDS-Scicon
Pembroke House, Pembroke Broadway
Camberley, Surrey GU15 3XD

Supplier in USA:

Electronic Data Systems
Technology Architecture
5400 Legacy Drive
Dallas, TX 75230

Key features:

The Apache toolset supports the collection of information on processes
with a pictorial language. It provides a range of approaches to map,
analyse, improve and automate the processes.

Methodology support:

The Apache toolset is used as part of EDS' Apache methodology.
The use of Apache is described in Gary Born's paper "Apache: a pictorial
CASE tool for Business Process Engineering".

Operating environment:

Apple Macintosh (4/40 upwards)

Interfaces to other tools:

Provides standard export interfaces to most Macintosh software.
    The following figure shows the pictorial representation used to capture
process descriptions during interviews with process owners. The main
flow of process events is vertical; branches to the right normally indicate
conditions or details about information processed.

Reservation clerk...Process Reservation Request

In this example, the initial icon indicates that a communication from a customer will cause a travel request to be initiated. The flight schedule is retrieved from its database, on a screen called Flgt-Sch.

In 15% of cases, no flight is available. For the other 85%, the flight is booked, and a travel request completed. This is filed, and a copy sent to the Support Clerk. The Flight Schedule screen is then deleted as it is no longer required.

BUSINESS DESIGN FACILITY (BDF)

Originator:

Texas Instruments, Inc.

Status:

Commercially available

Year of introduction:

1993

Price band:

Upper

Supplier in United Kingdom:

TI Information Engineering UK Ltd
(a Texas Instruments company)
European Headquarters
Wellington House, 61-73 Staines Road West
Sunbury-on-Thames TW15 1TZ
Tel: (+44) 784 245058 Fax: (+44) 932 770142

Supplier in USA:

Texas Instruments, Inc.
AIM Division, MS 8507
6620 Chase Oaks Boulevard
Dallas, TX 75023
Tel: (+1) 214 575 5599

Key features:

- Process modelling
- Organisational modelling
- Data modelling
- Flow modelling
- Model object interaction using matrices

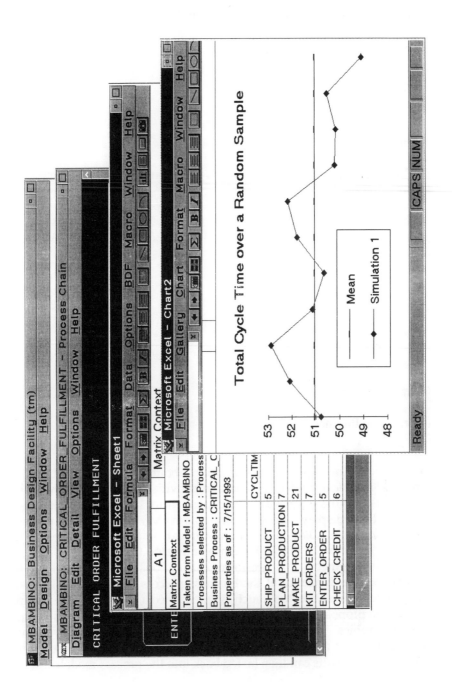

- Simulation and evaluation of existing and proposed designs
- Information Engineering support
- IDEF0 and IDEF1X support
- Model extensibility/customisation
- Model repository

Methodology support:

BDF is methodology neutral, and supports any generic Business Re-engineering method.

Continuous improvement of a process is supported.

The use of the BDF is described in Michael Mills and Clive Mabey's paper "Automating Business Process Re-engineering with the Business Design Facility".

Operating environments:

OS/2, Windows

Interfaces to other tools:

Information Engineering Facility (IEF)
DDE links

In the course of capturing information about the business, the BDF provides graphical models of data and activities, highlighting the tasks which make up the process and the dependencies between those tasks.

The BDF can display business operations in a variety of ways. A process can be viewed in isolation, or in any context, so that its relationship to other processes can be highlighted and understood.

Business engineers can perform calculations and simulations to understand the dynamics of the business process. Using BDF's links to analysis and calculation tools such as spreadsheets, the performance of an existing or proposed process can be simulated and displayed as values and in graphics. This allows you to understand where improvements are required and to test new designs to determine the optimal solution. Variables and results can then be fed back into the process model.

The BDF enables the practitioner to obtain all the critical information needed to evaluate the redesign alternatives for the business. This information can be integrated with spreadsheets or other tools, such as simulation and activity-based costing packages, to obtain statistics and evidence to validate performance measurements.

Metrics such as cost and cycle time can be used with any tasks and dependencies within the business model, and user-defined metrics can be introduced without any practical limit.

BUSINESS IMPROVEMENT FACILITY (BI*f*)

Originator:
Virtual Software Factory Ltd

Status: Commercially available

Year of introduction: 1993

Price band: Medium to upper (according to options)

Supplier in United Kingdom: Virtual Software Factory Ltd
                                       Crest House, Embankment Way
                                       Castleman Business Centre
                                       Ringwood, Hampshire BH24 1EU
                                       Tel: (+44) 425 474484 Fax: (+44) 425 474233

Supplier in USA: Virtual Software Factory, Inc.
                      13873 Park Center Road Suite 218
                      Herndon, Virginia, VA 22071
                      Tel: (+1) 703 318 1180 Fax: (+1) 703 318 1190

Key features: Enabling and support for:

*   Design and redesign of
    — Business processes
    — Manufacturing processes
    — Technical processes
*   IT requirements
*   People/human resource requirements

Suite of integrated methods supported by an integrated CASE tool, Meta CASE Foundation Product (Virtual Software Factory)

Methodology support:

BI*f* supports (IMPROVE) a business process modelling method (pioneered at National & Provincial Building Society in the UK), logical process modelling (RESOLVE), decision analysis (DECIDE) and resource specification (SPECIFY).
   Most other methods can be supported if required.

Operating environment:
OS/2, UNIX, ULTRIX, AIX and VMS (Windows 3.1 planned)

Interfaces to other tools:
RTM (Marconi Requirements Traceability Management)
ProcessWise (ICL Simulation & Process Enactment products)
Frame Maker, Desk Top Publishing

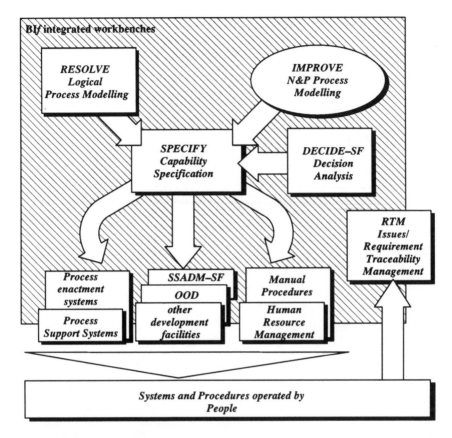

Interleaf, Desk Top Publishing
SSADM4-SF. SSADM4 CASE environment
TEXEL-SF, VIEWS-SF, OOA and OOD CASE environments
Any CDIF compatible tools

BI*f* is not just a tool as it embodies workbenches and methods for analysing, designing and re-engineering business processes.

BI*f* supports the progressive view of devoting a similar level of attention and effort to understanding and designing the processes of an organisation as to its systems. It therefore supports people, processes and systems modelling, and incorporates the concept of continual improvement. This then assumes change to be a normal part of the management process with systems designed to support people in this dynamic scenario.

BI*f* can be used for:

- Designing new organisations and supporting processes
- Redesigning critical processes
- Designing automation of processes
- Devising new 'people' roles and human resource policies
- Designing enterprise-wide data definitions and dictionaries

CADDIE

Originator:

Logica Cambridge Ltd

Status:

Research tool for consultancy support

Year of introduction:

1993

Price band:

On application

Supplier in United Kingdom:

Logica Cambridge Ltd
Betjeman House, 104 Hills Road
Cambridge CB2 1LQ

Supplier in USA:

None

Key features:

Object-oriented approach, support for explicit representation and use of organisational knowledge for modelling, support for sophisticated user defined performance evaluation metrics, open distributed multi-user architecture, well suited to strategy analysis and business gaming.

CADDIE is described in Faramarz Farhoodi's paper, "CADDIE: an advanced tool for organisational design and process modelling".

Methodology support:

Object-oriented design and programming

Operating environments:

Unix, X Windows, Sun SPARC

Interfaces to other tools:

Open object-oriented architecture facilitates interfacing to other tools.

Distributed Decision Modelling using CADDIE:

Distributed decision making requires close coordination and co-operation between staff with different responsibilities.

The complexity of the relationship between people in many environments makes the design of decision modelling systems very difficult.

Using CADDIE it will be possible to model:

- organisational structures and individual "agents" within the system (an agent is a special type of object that can sense, act and reason)
- task structures associated with decision making processes
- the means of communication used and the information exchanges involved
- the allocation and coordination of tasks between decision makers

CADDIE's agent-oriented approach to representation enriches the basic object-oriented paradigm and provides a highly flexible environment for modelling complex decision processes. An example CADDIE agent hierarchy is shown below. This diagram shows some of the different types of agents that can be defined in CADDIE and how they might be organised into classes and specialisations of these classes.

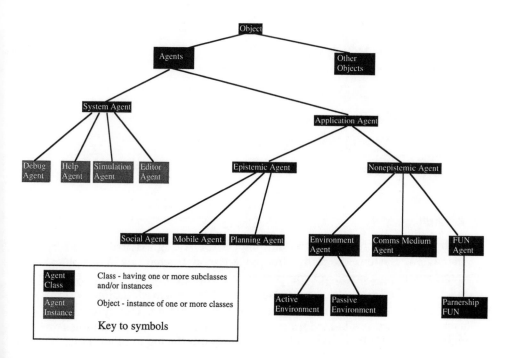

ithink

Originator:

High Performance Systems, Inc.

Status:

Commercially available

Year of introduction:

1989

Price band:

Lower to medium

Supplier in United Kingdom:

Cognitus Systems Ltd
1 Park View
Harrogate
North Yorkshire HG1 5LY
Tel: (+44) 423 562622 Fax: (+44) 423 567916

Supplier in USA:

High Performance Systems, Inc.
45 Lyme Road
Hanover, NH 03755

Key features:

ithink is a graphical process simulation tool designed to be used by managers. System diagrams (maps) are constructed via a graphical interface using a small yet comprehensive and wholly consistent symbol set. Quantified simulation models may then be constructed directly from system diagrams, without the need for programming. The dynamics of system and process behaviour may be exhibited in graphs and tables on the computer screen.

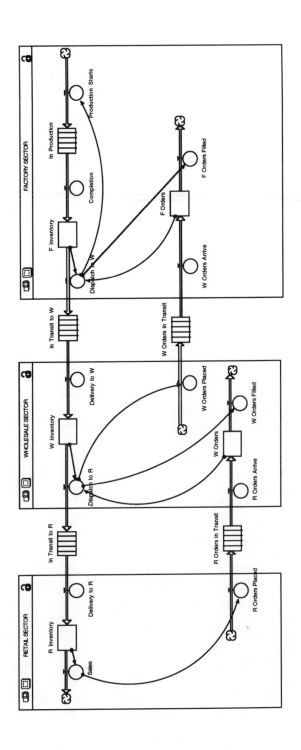

Methodology support:

System Dynamics
The structural basis and methodology are described in the paper by Richard Stevenson: "Strategic Process Engineering: a systems thinking approach using **ithink**".

Operating environments:

Apple Macintosh (Windows version available early 1994)

Interfaces to other tools:

Many other tools can be interfaced via the Macintosh system environment.

Example: Supply Chain Management:

In the example shown above, **ithink** has been used to represent a simple three-stage supply-chain process for an unspecified product. It may be seen that whereas physical goods flow down the supply chain, information (orders etc.) flows in the opposite direction.

Even simple supply-chain processes often exhibit quite complex behaviour (including demand and inventory amplification and oscillation) caused by interactions of decisions made by the *players* (factory, wholesaler, retailer) and the various delays within the system. Often, the overall cost and quality performance of such supply-chains may be far worse than the performance of which the process is capable.

Usually, each player within such a chain acts independently to maximise his own performance; decisions about (e.g.) inventory levels and re-order quantities are made locally. The frequent outcome is often that the *process as a whole* reacts in such a way as to frustrate and overturn the local decisions. Performance can be improved by understanding the overall *structure* of the process and by developing policies which manage the flow of goods and information across the organisational boundaries. Simulation is the *only* risk-free way to understand and to test the implications of different policy options.

ithink provides a visual methodology for charting process structure. **ithink** diagrams provide a rich vehicle for high-level discussion and debate, especially across functional and organisational boundaries. And because **ithink** diagrams can be transformed directly into simulation models, the dynamic behaviour and performance indicated by system and process structure can be quickly assessed.

ithink is a powerful design tool for high-level process engineering and an invaluable "front-end" to more detailed considerations of process management.

OBJECT MANAGEMENT WORKBENCH (OMW)

Originator:

Intellicorp Inc.

Status: Commercially available

Year of introduction: Introduced 1993

Price band: Upper

Supplier in United Kingdom: Intellicorp Ltd
Unit 6, Bracknell Beeches, Old Bracknell Lane West,
Bracknell, Berks, RG12 7BW

Supplier in USA: Intellicorp, Inc.
975 El Camino Real West
Mountain View, CA 94040 2216

Key features:

The OMW is a full life cycle CASE tool with executable diagrams that is well suited to Business Process Engineering. The Object Diagrammer allows the creation of object relationship diagrams which instantly create executable structures. The Business Rule Editor provides point and click, context sensitive construction of business rules and procedures which generate ANSII C code. The Event Diagrammer implements the operations, triggers and control conditions. The Scenario Manager takes test data and allows the diagrams to be animated, testing the business models that have been drawn. The tools Graphical User Interface builder allows end user interfaces to be built to support communication with business users.

Methodology support:

The OMW supports the Martin/Odell extended Information Engineering methodology which includes a spiral analysis and design approach. It supports the full development life cycle.

Operating environments:

The OMW runs on UNIX workstations with plans to offer PC based versions. The toolset which includes IntelliCorp's rapid application development tool, Kappa, is designed to produce applications in a standalone or distributed environment.

Interfaces to other tools:

The OMW can link with any tools which have a C application programmer's interface, and also supports direct links to SQL relational databases.

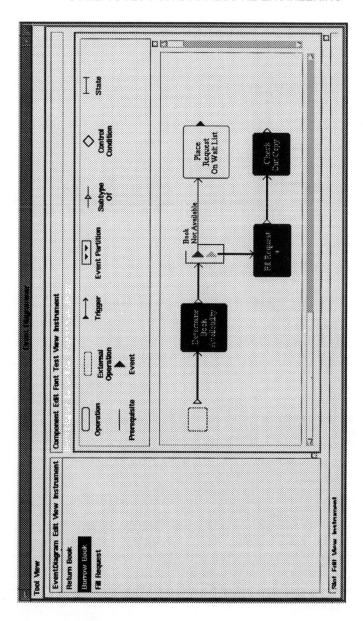

Active Diagrams Animate Designs

This diagram shows an Event diagram which has just completed an animation run. The notation is that of the Martin/Odell methodology.

Diagrams are instantly translated into working code which can then be executed, animating the diagrams. Instead of drawing passive diagrams and then writing code, the pictures are the code, and can be easily modified.

PROCESSWISE WORKBENCH

Originator:

International Computers Ltd

Status:

Commercially available

Year of introduction:

1993

Price band:

Prices are available on application to ICL

Supplier in United Kingdom:

Business Process Management Unit, ICL Enterprises
Forest Road, Feltham TW13 7ES
Tel: (+44) 81 890 1414 Fax: (+44) 81 893 2672

Supplier in USA:

ICL Business Systems
11490 Commerce Park Drive
Reston, VA 22091
Tel: (+1) 703 648 3300 Fax: (+1) 703 264 0319

Key features:

ProcessWise WorkBench is a business process modelling tool designed
to assist the business analyst in designing processes for maximum
performance within the overall critical success factors of the business.

ProcessWise WorkBench uses an intuitive style of representing and
analysing process flows which requires no IT skills on behalf of the business
analyst. This defines:

- who—people, roles, systems, or services,
- does what—activity, function, process, or task,
- to what—document, object, information, or product.

The WorkBench's powerful analysis tools are then used to evaluate the
efficiency and effectiveness of the process model (typically to identify

bottlenecks, resource requirements or usage and critical path routes) and to assess the impact of change.

ProcessWise WorkBench is driven by a fully extensible, object-oriented meta-model and a dynamic rule base, which makes it uniquely powerful and flexible.

The meta-model defines the configuration, in terms of process objects and their relationships, for each process model developed. The configurability of the meta-model extends to the visual attributes of diagrams, the information and objects in a process model, and to the analytical functions that may be invoked.

Rules are used to define how processes behave. These provide a simulation capability which "runs the rules" and supports "what if" analysis of metrics such as time, cost and resources. If the organisation's critical success factors can be defined as rules, they may be tested during simulation.

This rule-based approach enables full model integrity to be maintained. All objects, roles and relationships defined are rigorously checked. Each time the rule set is applied to the model completeness is assured. The rule base also provides support for impact analysis of changes to requirements including the cross-referencing of affected objects.

Methodology support:

The WorkBench can be used as a free-standing tool. Its use is also integral to the process capture and process modelling phases of ICL's Business Process Re-engineering methodology, ProcessWise Guide.

The configurability facilities of the rule base and meta-model referred to above are also used to enable the WorkBench to be easily configured to support any chosen process modelling and analysis method.

Operating environments:

Unix 5.4 or SUN SPARCstation systems, as stand-alone or networked systems. PCs running X-Vision can also act as client systems in client-server networks.

Interfaces to other tools:

CDIF interfaces are provided to enable process and data model information to be transferred to CASE products which support structured systems analysis and design methods.

ProcessWise WorkBench is also capable of generating code to drive ICL's process support system, ProcessWise Integrator.

RADitor

Originator: Co-ordination Systems Ltd

Status: Commercially available

Year of introduction: 1993

Price band: Lower

Supplier in United Kingdom: Co-ordination Systems Ltd
3c Cornbrash Park, Bumpers Way
Chippenham, Wiltshire SN14 6RA
Tel: (+44) 249 448870 Fax: (+44) 249 448200

Supplier in USA: None

Key features:

An Activity Editor provides drawing business processes as Role Activity Diagrams. These diagrams are described in "Process Modelling—Why, What and How" by Tim Huckvale and Martyn Ould.

Notes can be added to all process elements.

A built-in Questionnaire facilitates structured interviews and records responses.

A forecaster is being prototyped to model activity time, staff and resource costs.

A co-ordination system supports workflow and procedure tracing.

Process descriptions form the basis for process enactment, enabling context sensitive use of multi-vendor applications, such as database systems, spreadsheets and word-processors.

The process library can form the basis of control for a quality management system.

Methodology support:

The RADit method is used to derive models of an organisation's key processes. Models developed using the Activity Editor may form the basis of a procedures manual, can be used for Activity Based Costing, and for determining where business processes are best supported by computer systems.

Operating environment: Windows

Interfaces to other tools:

Notes and diagrams can be exported for use with Windows based applications.

Role Activity Diagrams (RADs) produced by the Activity Editor are more than pictures. Each RAD forms a framework on which to hang properties such as text, time values, resource costs and volumes, and even

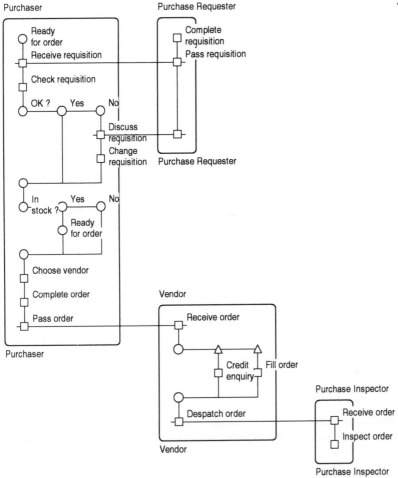

computer applications which can be used to automate and enact a process.

A role is a sequence of steps undertaken by a single person or department. In the purchasing example below, there are four roles:

- Purchase Requester, who asks for something to be purchased
- Purchaser, who places orders
- Vendor, who supplies things for purchase
- Purchase Inspector, who checks the goods on arrival

There is no firm correspondence between people and roles. One person may perform more than one role, for example, the purchasing officer may be both Purchaser and Inspector.

In the example, the Purchaser checks to see whether the items requested are already in stock. If they are, the process is complete. Thus, the *yes* thread contains a state node labelled *Ready for order*, which also occurs at the top of the role. Thus, the role jumps back to the top, and is ready to begin the process again. Otherwise, the role, and the process, continues.

SES/WORKBENCH

Originator:

Scientific and Engineering Software

Status: Commercially available

Year of introduction: 1988

Price band: Upper

Supplier in United Kingdom: Scientific and Engineering Software UK Ltd
Corinthian Court, Milton Park
Abingdon OX14 4RY
Tel: (+44) 235 861321 Fax: (+44) 235 861320

Supplier in USA: Scientific and Engineering Software, Inc.
4301 Westbank Drive
Austin, TX 78746

Key features:

Behavioural modelling and simulation of systems and processes
Performance and dynamic visualisation

Methodology support:

Performance modelling—queuing theory, resources, parallel processes, task synchronisation, and others.

Operating environments:

UNIX on Sun SPARC, IBM RS/6000, HP700, DEC ULTRIX

Interfaces to other tools:

Automatic links to existing code in C, PASCAL, FORTRAN, etc.
CADRE's Teamwork and IDE's StP, for transfer of RTSA models
VHDL for output to hardware VHDL tools

This submodel represents the customer perception of what happens inside a high street bank. This simple model illustrates some typical SES/Workbench concepts.
There are some resources:

- manager and clerks—active resources
- withdrawal slips and payment forms—passive resources

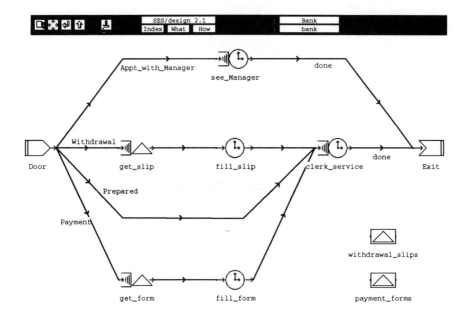

There are some 'processes':

- get_slip; fill_slip
- get_form; fill_form
- see_Manager and clerk_service

The bank's customers represent the workload for this model. All customers enter the bank through the door. Depending on what type of service each customer requires, they will take one of four different arcs.

If they have an appointment to see the manager, they enter a queue to wait. When the manager is free, he/she will see the next customer in line. There is probably only one manager in each branch office. It then takes a certain amount of time to have a meeting with the manager, after which the customer leaves.

Other customers might want to make withdrawals or payments. Some will already have their forms prepared, so they can go straight into the queue to wait for a clerk.

Others will have to take a form and fill it out before joining the queue.

There might be three clerks on duty. The person at the front of the queue goes to the first free clerk, etc.

Queues in banks tend to be mostly "single queue/multiple server" but it is just as easy to model "multiple queue/single server" and "multiple queue/multiple server".

TOP-IX

Status: Commercially available

Year of introduction: 1989 (Continuous upgrade path)

Price band: Process Management Modules—from under £500 per user
  Analysis System (depends on options) £1600 to £9000 per user

Supplier in United Kingdom: TOP-IX Ltd
  Falstaff House, 33 Birmingham Road
  Stratford-upon-Avon, Warwickshire CV37 0AZ
  Tel: (+44) 789 414642 Fax: (+44) 789 261165

Representative in USA: John Bradbury
  10870 Jennifer Marie Place
  Fairfax Station, VA 22039
  Tel: (+1) 703 978 7507

Key features:

Process Analysis and Design Features:

- Powerful MS Windows based process mapping
- Top-down process decomposition
- Process documentation
- Value-added analysis—eliminates wasted effort
- Cycle time analysis—reduces delays
- Human resources and costs directly linked to processes and volumes of business
- Powerful Relational Data Base Management System (RDBMS) simplifies both process and corporate modelling of costs and resources

Process Management features:

- Customisable reporting
- Detailed staff planning for volume forecasts
- Budgeting
- Activity based costing
- Performance monitoring
- Detailed work scheduling
- Staff absences and peak loads considered
- Customer priorities considered
- Staff skills balance and training needs reports